MISSISSIPPI

MISSISSIPPI

Text by
Bern Keating

Photographs by
Franke Keating

 UNIVERSITY PRESS OF MISSISSIPPI *Jackson*

**For John,
and the children
of Mississippi**

First Printing, 1982
Second Printing, 1983
Third Printing, 1984

Library of Congress Cataloging in Publication Data

Keating, Bern.
  Mississippi.

  1. Mississippi—Description and travel—
1981-   —Views. I. Keating, Franke. II. Title.
F342.K4 1982   917.62'0463   82-11122
ISBN 0-87805-165-1

*Grappling with a knotty intellectual
problem, the author fights his way to a
solution in the approved Mississippi
manner . . . while Mme. Photographer
spurns the down-to-earth for a Mississippi
high.*

Contents

Introduction

Beginning with a childhood spent roaming a land crammed with fuzzy nestlings, acres of wildflowers, frisky colts, plodding turtles, spotted fawns, the Mississippian spends his life wrapped about with the homely wonders of this pretty little planet's natural world.

YEARS AGO, while I was still a new Mississippian, I was picking at an avocadoburger on a California patio and struggling to understand the cocktail party small talk which was simple enough but was spoken in the coastal dialect. The host's daughter put the standard question asked of strangers at any American party.

"Where are *you* coming from . . . geographicallywise, that is?"

"Mississippi."

"But you seem like a nice intelligent man," she protested. "Who can you relate to in that intellectual desert?" She was genuinely distressed for me. "I mean, do you ever rap with anybody but Neanderthalers out there?"

In those days, I was still an unduly sensitive Mississippian, but I remembered in time that we were renowned for our courtly manners.

"Well, I've talked with some pretty able troglodytes lately," I answered in gentle tones. Then I dropped on her a load of names shrewdly calculated to shake up a California girl.

I told her that for Christmas dinner at my house in Greenville, we had the company of Karl Malden, Mildred Dunnock, Ira Wallach and Carroll Baker.

Because she was a college student and presumably familiar with American literature, I let her have another barrel. I told her that the cinema stars had wanted to hear about the chaps we had recently met at Hodding Carter's place, like the poets Robert Penn Warren or Robert Tristram Coffin. Then there was the South African revolutionary novelist Alan Paton who stayed with me while he studied the South. Or, James Jones who blew in riding a van escorted by a squad of outriders on motorcycles.

"Oh, wow," she philosophized. "I *am* sorry. That crowd probably is brighter even than this California bunch, I guess."

Her pretty contrition was disarming, but she had surrendered too soon, before I had tossed in front of her the names of our native Mississippi

While the men fought to subdue a wilderness, the women nurtured the civilizing arts, so that, once the forest was conquered, Mississippi discovered that life here was not only possible but downright good.

Revisionists stubbornly try to demolish the myths about Mississippi's Deep South culture, but one romantic legend remains indestructibly true: the women down here are stunning.

brains and artists—the Eudora Weltys, Walker Percys, Ellen Douglases, Willie Morrises, Shelby Footes, Hodding Carters, Leontyne Prices, B.B. Kings, and Craig Claibornes that a practiced Mississippi name-dropper keeps in his bag.

Nevertheless, my confounding of the young woman's innocent provincialism by dropping the names of celebrated visitors to my home state was not really cheating. Perhaps the greatest single charm of Mississippians is an unbridled hospitality that brings more dazzling benefits to the host than to the guest.

Like any other outlanders, we brighten our leisure with a steady procession from urban centers of cultural aides like lecturers, poets, painters, pianists, ballet stars, and barber shop quartets. Unlike other regions however, we are not content to sit passively through their tricks for an evening, abandoning them afterward to a plastic supper in a lonely motel. A Mississippian's first impulse on confronting a new outbreak of the Black Death would be to throw a party, so he certainly cannot pass up the chance to force a tumbler of bourbon and a plate of quail on a visiting celebrity.

Thus, we have enriched our lives over the years by cram feeding our brilliant visitors, who have unwittingly but cheerfully sung for their suppers and left behind as a bread-and-butter present a small piece of their artists' souls which we have tucked into our private treasure store.

Listening to a Northern friend outlining plans for a new house, my wife was horrified when the Yankee girl chuckled with grim satisfaction that she had carefully omitted any space for overnight guests. Never is my household, or any Mississippi household, livelier than when the lady of the house is humming as she snaps fresh sheets on the guest room beds and lays out pallets on the floor for the overflow of expected visitors.

It's the women, after all, who make Mississippi worthwhile. They are endlessly astonishing in their mixture of ladylike delicacy and rocklike resistance to life's inescapable catastrophes. The imperturbable Miss Emily in William Faulkner's great short story "A Rose for Emily"—the maiden lady who serenely dismissed the town councilmen with the unshakeable assertion that she had never paid taxes and wasn't about to begin—is far from a baseless invention. Our local grande dame, hauled into city court for ignoring a raft of parking tickets big enough to piece a double bed quilt, routed the city prosecutor with the argument that common law and the Constitution forbid the use of police power to raise revenue. The judge whispered to the bailiff to get her out of the courtroom before her seditious truths perverted innocent eavesdroppers. She never received another ticket and would have ignored it anyhow.

If you get into bad trouble, you must try to do it amongst Mississippi women for they are bottomless reservoirs of strength and love to carry you through the hard parts.

When our daughter died, our friends found us working on the Florida coast and, because of my high blood pressure, arranged for a doctor to be present when they broke the terrible news to us. A friend sent his private plane to carry us home. Another friend stayed behind to drive our car back. Still another quietly took over the dreary details of getting her body home from distant Quebec and making the funeral arrangements.

Meanwhile, a company of gentle women took over the household, prepared meals for out-of-town mourn-

Among those women, some had the God-given talent to share with the world the slyly amused and infinitely compassionate view of their neighbors that their sisters held in secret. Over those gifted few, Eudora Welty reigns as queen.

9

ers, arranged for their shelter, ministered to our needs, comforted us as best they could through our devastating grief. For days, we had no duties but to grapple with the problem of facing life without Kate. We could not have done it without Mississippi women.

Besides their natural kindliness, those Mississippi women also have high respect for strictly formal manners. They teach their children the kind of etiquette that went out elsewhere with the disciplinary woodshed visit. Mississippi youngsters routinely address their elders as "Sir" and "Ma'am" and often stand when adults enter the room.

Throughout the North, visiting Mississippi youngsters get away with murder because Northern hostesses are enchanted—stunned—by their manners. My close women friends—old enough to be grandparents themselves—retain those formal folkways and address me gravely as "Sir." I like it. And so does everybody else, North and South.

There must be something in the air that softens the female vocal chords. One of the most effective of the Mississippi girl's charms is the famous dulcet voice of the Southern belle. But even before the modern Mississippi woman's arrival, early European travelers re-

So that Mississippi's child will not spend a totally deprived youth, an occasional winter lets drop a meager fall of snow, just enough for a single day's romp with a sled which should last 10 lifetimes.

On the same latitude as the Sahara, Mississippi welcomes spring one day and summer the next, giving youngsters most of a year to spend in the long lazy days when the whole world is incubating under the hot sun. Eve's granddaughter relishes her apple and a romance under a flowering crape myrtle; an equestrienne broods over the mystery of a gloomy cypress brake; sisters in crackling new springtime frocks gambol through a field where once a squirrel could not pass without courting death; a beautiful young Choctaw graces the landscape at summer's Indian Fair.

11

According to the mood of the moment, young folk can make bold explorations of the wilderness or of hidden corners of the home neighborhood.

marked on the voices of the Indian women of the region which they described as "very agreeable to the ears, courteous, gentle . . . so fine and musical as to represent the singing of birds." For a Choctaw village of old or a Chi Omega soiree at Ole Miss of today, the description still holds.

Also Mississippians aren't homogenized into plastic clones of drearily predictable reactions. Not yet.

Where else would I find a boarding house lady who took a nap during the first landing on the moon because "if God had of wanted folks to be on the moon, he'd of borned them there."

Or the lady who carried two big cans of black-eyed peas to a monster New Year's Day rally in Vienna for fear some of the other Mississippi visitors had forgotten to bring their own peas. Long tradition dictates that every Mississippian must eat at least a mouthful to start the year off right, so her steaming silver bowl was greeted with great cries of relief from the fellow expatriates she found at that Austrian rout.

Or my sometime gardener who won't put in the spring garden any day but Good Friday, probably with some dim religious idea of putting death in the ground in the expectation of resurrected life.

I moved to Mississippi right after Navy service in World War II. Since then, I have worked in something like 120 countries. My entire factory is the size of a ballpoint pen. We can live anywhere we want. And sometimes, we have been tempted. While working in Santa Fe, Paris, San Francisco, New Orleans, or New York, we have asked ourselves why we stay on in a state about as remote from my writer's market as I could find. Then, we hang about our new love one day too long. And we desperately miss our Mississippi home.

Because Mississippi has juice, flavor, color, scent . . . it has what only a Mississippi word can define.

It has *suption.*

During sensuous outings at the arts in the evening or at a gastronomic blowout on a sunny afternoon, life in Mississippi has a savor that can be defined only by a word that is peculiar to Mississippi. It has suption.

13

CHAPTER 1

The Living Has Been Mostly Easy

WHILE THE WESTERN COASTAL red men were digging roots with their fingernails, our Natchez Indians had developed the highest aboriginal civilization north of the Valley of Mexico. Perhaps the region's moderate climate and gentle diversity of environment gave the early arrivals a lift on the road to high living. Located roughly between 30° and 35° north latitude, Mississippi is about as far from the equator and the pole as the balmy Madeira Islands, the Holy Lands, the Great Pyramid of Cheops, and the fabled Vale of Kashmir.

The first arrivals didn't have to spend their lives fighting up and down rocky slopes, for the highest point is in Tishomingo County where the Appalachian range dies away at 806 feet.

The annual rainfall of about fifty-two to fifty-five inches is matched in the United States only by the other Gulf regions and South Carolina . . . and the Alaska Panhandle, of course, where a sunny day excites dancing in the streets.

Early Mississippians found the woods and prairies swarming with game—deer, bear, wildcat, wolf and cougar, beaver, mink and otter, fox, rabbit, squirrel, raccoon, and opossum. The wood bison was killed off, probably even before the white man arrived. The beaver was also trapped out, but has returned in enough numbers to plague farmers by its hatred of the sound of running water. The furry engineers flood thousands of acres of prime farmland by their frenzied construction of mud and timber dams.

Hernando de Soto, the first European to visit Mississippi, found the red men to be skillful farmers with a high standard of living for a Stone Age people. It was the advanced culture of the Mississippi tribes that got them into trouble with de Soto. They had laid in stores of maize for winter feasting. De Soto and his conquistadors believed in living off the land, by which they meant living off the goods they stole from anybody silly enough to work for a living. Unfortunately for them, the Chickasaws of North

Of course, there is no such thing as enough ducks for a true hunter, but it is significant that wood ducks are considered to be pests because they clutter up a clear shot at the mallards.

*Sportsmen who resort to guerilla tactics that could
undermine entrenched empires are regularly
frustrated by turkeys that outguess all their
tricks though armed with a brain no larger than
a filbert.*

Mississippi were a manly and warlike lot who were
loath to give up the corn their women had labored
over so long in the sun-blasted fields. They gave the
conquistadors a very hard time. When de Soto came
up against the Mississippi River, he hastened to build
rafts so he could flee across the waters, though equally
hostile tribes threatened him from the other shore.

That historic spot where in 1541 the Spanish gang-
ster first saw the Mississippi, incidentally, is the proud
possession of a half dozen Mississippi river landings.
In 1938, a presidential commission solemnly decided
de Soto saw the river at Sunflower Landing, north of
Rosedale. Other claimants, with some justification,
scorn the effort to pinpoint an event that took place in
an uncharted jungle 400 years ago.

Great and complex civilizations, only slightly more
backward than the impressive Toltec and Aztec cultures of Mexico, had flourished in Mississippi for centuries, but had mysteriously disappeared shortly before
the first white colonizers came, 150 years after de Soto.
Those vanished priest-kings and their subjects had left
the tribes that followed them more than a smattering
of their culture, however, and the Mississippi tribes
had not reverted to hunting and gathering but had continued to till their maize and beans and squash.

The Natchez people had even clung to a considerable
part of the elaborate social organization and technological skills, artistic vigor, and ritualized religion—all
clearly borrowed from Mexico—that had once made
the Mound Builders among the most advanced people
of the New World.

Those cultured aborigines obviously knew a good
thing when they saw it and were quick to borrow from
distant civilizations, white or red, for the first colonizers into the region found that two of the thirteen lunar
months had already been named for the peach and
watermelon, two Old World fruits that had only recently been introduced to the New World by Span-
iards on the distant Atlantic Coast of Florida. Somehow, Mississippi's Indian farmers had bought or stolen
seeds and saplings of the exotics, so that two of modern Mississippi's favorite fruits were awaiting arrival of
European settlers.

Ownership of the state passed back and forth between England, France, Spain, and the United States in
a bewildering series of Old World treaties. The pow-
dered and periwigged diplomats of Europe scuffled for
a foothold on the lower banks of the Mississippi so
they could tax the commerce of half a continent floating down the stream to the sea.

But somewhere on the Mississippi's banks during
that time, just before the eighteenth turned to the nineteenth century, a tough woods runner, clad in buck-
skin, parted the tangled cane stalks with his rifle barrel, spat into the stream, and laid final claim to the
land.

The true owner had arrived, the first of the land-
hungry English-speaking colonists crowded off the Atlantic seaboard looking for a home. In a dazzlingly short
time, they had poured into what was then called the
Southwest Frontier.

By 1817 Mississippi was a state, the 20th admitted

16

For a state that lies mostly inland, water gleams somewhere in the background of most revelries—bayous, lakes, rivers, oxbows, farm ponds, and the vast impoundments that make up Mississippi's "Great Lakes" glitter enticingly under the slanting rays of the sun.

18

When the lakes freeze over up north, the keenest yachtsmen flee to Mississippi's shallow sunbowl between the mainland coast and the offshore islands.

For the price of a wire basket and a length of clothesline, coastal folk furnish the table with sea fare that would crack an oil magnate's expense account at a northern city restaurant. And in Mississippi it will arrive at the table almost still kicking.

Along the coast, the state's vaunted hospitality has become a profession and the care, feeding and pampering of the visitor is the round-the-clock concern of the entire population.

20

to the Union. The state covers 47,716 square miles and is 32nd of the 50 states in area, being slightly smaller than Louisiana, slightly larger than Pennsylvania and one-twelfth the size of Alaska. Its mean length is 340 miles, about the same distance as the whole length of the British Isles where most of Mississippi's ancestors originated. Its mean width is 170 miles, somewhat more than Northern Ireland where all the first Mississippians named McSomething came from.

The geographic center of the state is nine miles WNW of Carthage.

Geologists have divided the state into many regions according to their arcane science which is more concerned with what happened a billion years ago than what hits the eye today. Most modern travelers distinguish the dwindling foothills of the Appalachian mountains in the northeast, the Black Prairie near the Alabama border in the central belt, the Delta flatlands from Memphis to Vicksburg, the Piney Woods forests in the south-central, the bluffs along the Lower Mississippi, and the Coast.

Mississippi barely has a coast—only 44 miles of true shoreline. It may be more than New Hampshire's puny 13 miles or Delaware's 28 or Maryland's 31 miles, but it is pretty small stuff compared to Alaska's 5,580. Nevertheless, coastal dwellers will match their sugar sand beach and barrier islands against the finest beach resorts Delaware or Maryland can offer . . . or Alaska either, for that matter.

The state probably has the most colorful history of any in the Union, including Massachusetts or Virginia.

In the last year of the seventeenth century, Frenchmen established the first permanent settlement in the Mississippi Valley at what is now Ocean Springs. Spanish, British, and American flags followed. And for four years during the tragic fraternal struggle that almost destroyed the Union, the Confederate flag enjoyed the allegiance of Mississippians though it had been driven, by midway in the war, from the riverbank and coast and much of the interior.

The agonies of that useless bloodletting are undeniable. But the sufferings of the defeated people during the Reconstruction period may have been enhanced by the histrionic complaints of a populace skilled at story telling and the creation of legends.

The state saw hard times during the great flood in 1927 and during the Great Depression of the 1930's. But the most agonizing period was the strife that went with the immense racial adjustments of the late 1950's and the 1960's. Tensions became truly ugly and blood was shed before massive resistance to the new age of racial relations collapsed.

Today Mississippi has more black elected officials than any other state in the Union. Small-town black

Even the transatlantic yacht racers advertised as speeding toward the finish line at New Orleans slyly put in at Gulfport and finish the trip on wheels. You can't beat that recommendation for yachting waters.

mayors abound. Virtually any city council is going to have at least one black member. School boards are often black dominated.

In the state where bloody riots resisted the entry of black James Merideth to the University of Mississippi, the board that regulates all public advanced education is now headed by a black man.

Pockets of segregation still exist in private clubs and schools, but the bitterness of racial conflict has long since mellowed to at least tolerance and often a guarded fellowship in pursuit of some community project of mutual benefit.

The warm genuine friendship between many whites and blacks, usually based on long proximity at work, still goes on as it has for almost two centuries, regardless of the state of racial relations in the general community.

And then there is the considerable percentage of Mississippians who at heart really don't care what color anybody is and find the whole subject tiresome. In them, perhaps, lies the best hope for the future.

Mississippi cherishes its artists. Sometimes, like Willie Morris, they make it big elsewhere and come home again. At Laurel, they grab what local art they can rescue from the world market and add it to the astounding collection of world masters they hoard in their art gallery. And in a remote cornfield, a boy coaxes music from a flute made in the style of his Choctaw ancestors.

22

If the Gulf Coast's only rugby team can celebrate defeat so joyously, what would they do if they ever won a game?

Creative artists—one creates new plants to feed the world's starving, the other creates beauty to feed the soul. Each a creative artist—Dr. Edgar Hartwig creating new soybean strains at the Stoneville Experiment Station, a young potter creating Shearwater designs at Ocean Springs.

Amidst the jazzy bistros and pleasure domes of the Coast are a few quiet retreats of surpassing elegance.

27

CHAPTER 2

The Eponymous River

AS NEARLY AS historians can tell, the river and the state take the name Mississippi from two Chippewa Indian words meaning, if you are poetically bent, "Father of the Waters." Or, more prosaically and probably more realistically, "heap big river."

The Mississippi has loomed over the state's history from the days when the first French explorers and voyageurs traveled it in their canoes.

As though the fates knew of the tremendous destiny awaiting steamboats, the voyage of the *New Orleans*, first steamboat to navigate the river, was attended by prodigious events. Instead of just plodding downstream from Pittsburgh to New Orleans, a voyage historic enough for any puny 116-footer, the doughty little boat first acted as lying-in hospital for the birth of the captain's child. And just days later, the boat was tossed about in the gigantic convulsions of the New Madrid Earthquake, the most horrendous upheaval to hit the crust of North America in historic times.

With nerves of steel, Captain Roosevelt survived the two events, about equally tumultuous to a young father, and steamed on to show that the era of current-driven flatboats had ended and the day of steam had dawned. He arrived in New Orleans in the first days of 1812.

Soon the steamboat world was invested with more glamour than space travel enjoys today. To become a pilot was the goal of small boy dreams. The dining halls became the ultimate in North American rococo luxury, rivalling the banquet halls of European palaces. Aboard the *City of Memphis*, a printing press turned out a daily newspaper for the passengers. The *Belle Creole* was reputedly so luxurious that the kitchen crew scorned to wash the china; they simply threw it overboard after every meal. Menus were staggeringly long and loaded not only with imported delicacies but also with choice game brought aboard as a gift by planters who rode free as a come-on for their cotton shipping trade. One steamboat set a record by carrying 9,200 bales in a single load.

The great river that gives the state its name bears more commerce today than in the grandest days of the paddlewheel steamboats. A single tow can haul as much cargo as a freight train that would reach from the terminal in one major city to the station of another city in another county.

Ironically, the Union's generals understood better than the Confederate president, who farmed a plantation within sight of Vicksburg, that control of the great river meant victory or defeat. Now, young Mississippians wonder at the monuments honoring those who bled on the river's banks to determine who should rule the channels.

To navigate rivers that rose and fell with astounding speed, boats became ever more powerful and shallower in draft. Only a decade or so after their first appearance, they paddled up incredibly shallow streams and made unnecessary the building of highways.

On narrow bayous far from the big river, plantation chatelaines shopped for china aboard crockery boats, courting couples had their likenesses struck on daguerreotype boats, and rustic audiences made their first encounter with culture at melodramas on showboats. Paddlewheelers towing barges to double their capacity hauled all the freight of the teeming mid-continent.

A cruise down the river from Memphis to the Louisiana line passes milepost after milepost distinguished by some event in steamboat history.

Mile 716.2. At Norfolk Landing, straddling the Tennessee-Mississippi boundary, the Confederate States of America in 1861 set up a customs checkpoint. Notices published in newspapers up and down the river notified steamboat captains that southbound boats (presumably coming from Yankee country, which seems odd, for it implies open trade with the enemy) were required to stop for a permit to land cargoes downstream in Confederate territory.

Steamboat captains were accustomed to being the absolute monarchs of their little domains, and so they were enraged by the new Republic's sticking its nose into their business. Hundreds of river dwellers, who cared little about other issues involved in that hideous struggle, were sufficiently outraged by distant Richmond's efforts to regulate their movements on their river that they joined the Union. To them the four-year bloodletting was a fight to reopen the river to unfettered steamboating.

Mile 658. Here General U.S. Grant tried one of his characteristically bold moves that occasionally brought him victory but always brought acute misery to anybody in his vicinity.

Before man began tinkering with the river, a dinky little bayou called Yazoo Pass connected Moon Lake

and the big stream. The stubborn river kept punching holes through early dikes, but in 1859 local planters put up a levee sturdy enough to keep the waters out.

Frustrated by the impregnable waterfront fortress at Vicksburg, Grant was obsessed with the idea of taking the Mississippi "Gibraltar" from the landward side. He cut through the Yazoo Pass levee and sent a flotilla of tinclads and transports by way of Moon Lake into the Coldwater and Tallahatchie Rivers with the idea of reaching the Yazoo and landing troops behind the river city's defenses.

Confederate troops cut trees and dropped their trunks across the narrow channel. Snipers picked off the Union soldiers wielding axes to clear the way and in the best guerilla tradition melted away into the Delta swamps when the Union landing parties stormed ashore.

Just upstream from Greenwood, at a sharp bend in the narrow river, the Confederates set up a few field pieces behind a crude earthworks, called it Fort Pemberton, and blasted the head of the Union naval column when it hove into view. Already short of temper because of the wickedly narrow and crooked channels they had been navigating, Union officers cursed the hornet's nest at the bend of the Tallahatchie River and turned back to the Mississippi.

Meanwhile, another Union column coming up the same tangled network of rivers and bayous from the south ran into a company of irregular calvary from Greenville, dug in atop an Indian mound on Rolling Fork. In an encounter between horsemen and warships, rare in the annals of warfare, the Union relief flotilla was driven off.

Mile 638.5 At Island No. 63 near Humber, Rebels shot up a passing Union steamboat. United States soldiers landed on both banks of the mainland. Because they could not catch the elusive bushwhackers, they acted like soldiers of all nations and times by laying waste the countryside, burning barns, houses, and crops of local farmers without inquiring into innocence or guilt. Late in the war, Admiral Porter set up a wood-yard on the island to refuel his river navy. Slaves liberated from the cotton fields found themselves pressed into Union service cutting and hauling firewood. Admiral Porter was enraged to discover that the ungrateful black freedmen apparently found little difference between being forced to pick cotton or compelled to cut firewood, for they had conspired with their former masters to pack gunpowder into hollow logs with the hope of blowing up a few Yankee boilers.

Mile 625. The river near Rena Lara comes closest to where the Washington commission pundits decided de Soto saw the stream. The river in 1942 took a short cut across the narrow neck of Sunflower Bend and isolated Sunflower Landing but left the old bend as Lake de Soto, one of the dozens of beautiful crescent-shaped lagoons the meandering river has dropped along its course over the centuries.

Mile 560.5. Near Scott, at 6:30 in the morning of April 21, 1927, the levee burst and the raging river poured through to flood vast areas of the lowland Delta in the gravest natural catastrophe to hit Mississippi in modern times.

Mile 543. Spanish Moss Bend across Archer Island from Greenville, marks the farthest northern point where grows the picturesque air plant, related to the pineapple and the favorite symbol of artists trying to impart a spooky Southern romanticism to their works.

Mile 537.2. The present city of Greenville sits on the fourth site in its short history. The first two a few miles downstream were devoured by the river. The third was a bustling riverport when the Union navy captured the river as far as Vicksburg. The unvan-

32

Boots and hoofs wore down the Natchez Trace that ran from the farthest outpost of eastern civilization at Nashville to the Southwest Frontier at Natchez. Mixed with the hard-bitten frontiersmen, the bandits, and the fugitives were a core of pious settlers and pioneer churchmen who brought the gentling influence of the church to the new settlements. Today, the haunt of river pirates and defenses against invaders are toys for kids and avenues of commerce.

Along its banks, the river has scattered lovely
relics of its ancient ways—tranquil oxbow lakes
and the ruins of a cotton civilization it once
nurtured.

And in its riverports thrived a curious little tribe
of folk who made the telling of stories about that
river culture their reason for living, like Ellen
Douglas whose novels rarely wander far from the
sound of the stream's running waters.

34

quished city sheltered Rebel sharpshooters who fired on passing Union river traffic. The Union Navy burned Greenville in retaliation.

During World War II, three river men, Jesse Brent, G.G. McCool, and Percy LeMay, brought to Greenville from Vicksburg a dinky 330-horsepower wooden-hulled towboat named *Gilder Faye*. Today Greenville is the Liberia of the inland waterways with a huge fleet based there—more than 100 towboats and 300 barges—and the offices of the river's major towing companies.

Mile 526. Officially called American Bend, this crook in the river near Avon was always called Shirt Tail Bend by the riverboat trade because of the casual costumes worn by the laborers in an immense wood-yard maintained there for refueling of steamboats. When the river sliced across the neck during the great flood of 1858, the abandoned channel became modern Lake Lee, one of the prettiest of the river's oxbows. The cub pilot of the first steamboat to attempt up-stream passage of the new channel was a certain Samuel Langhorne Clemens. He writes of his defeat by the still roaring cutoff currents in *Life on the Mississippi*.

Mile 437.1. The loss of Vicksburg by the Confederacy was the end of the war, but distant Richmond, infatuated by the glamour of the Eastern Establishment, refused to recognize defeat and continued the ghastly bloodletting for another futile two years.

The failure of the Confederate high command to defend Vicksburg properly is all the more puzzling because at Mile 415.5 lies Davis Island, an immense plantation worked by Jefferson Davis, the Confederacy's only president, and his brother. After the war, his brother recovered much of his confiscated land by swearing that he had never supported Jefferson's ambitions. Jefferson scorned to beg his enemies for favors and turned his back on his former lands.

Mile 389. After the fall of Vicksburg, the Union navy stationed a tinclad, the USS *Rattler*, on the river-bank at Rodney. Admiral Porter had good reason to distrust all the riverbank populace and ordered his sail-ors not to go ashore in towns unoccupied by federal troops.

Overcome by equal parts of piety and boredom, twenty-five officers and men one Sunday ignored his orders and filed into the Presbyterian church for serv-ices. Somebody scuttled into the woods to alert a company of Confederate guerillas. Not respecting the traditional rights of sanctuary in a church, they sur-rounded the building and poked guns through the doors and windows, capturing the unarmed sailors.

A humiliated Porter had the town bombarded. The church still shows marks where it was struck by can-nonballs.

The river gradually slid westward away from Rod-ney. Today it is a ghost town three miles from the river which gave it life.

Or like Ben Wasson who was godfather to a thousand talents, not the least of which was the state's greatest voice—William Faulkner.

Mile 363.8. Even before laying out New Orleans, the French built a fort on the heights at Natchez. The fort fell into ruins, and the city was not defended during the Civil War, so that a wealth of antebellum mansions still stands there. The ladies of Natchez have taken their antiquarian treasures in hand and with extraordinary shrewdness have managed them more economically and with more effect than any other historical preservation project in North America.

Mile 357.5. In 1942 a sad historic event took place when the steamboat *Tennessee Belle* caught fire and ran aground on Natchez Island. The crew stepped ashore and carried the boat's whistle with them back upstream to Natchez-under-the-Hill where they toasted the disappearance of the last steam packet on the Mississippi River.

Mile 305. The state's share of the great river ends at the Louisiana Line.

Left out of this history is the depressing litany of steamboat catastrophes. At virtually every bend and milepost on certain stretches of the river, some steamboat blew its boiler and sank, throwing hideously scalded passengers and crew into the treacherous stream. A significant percentage of the boilers gave way under the demands laid on them by a captain trying to win a race against a rival, though racing was frowned on or downright illegal.

Yet, even today river dwellers are in awe of the few surviving steamboats. When the *Delta Queen* and the *Mississippi Queen* tie up at the riverbank, Southern townfolk flock down to gaze at them in wonder. They are no less in awe of the splendid gimcrackery, the potent driving rod, and crimson sternwheel on the hundredth visit than on the first.

A century after its heyday a paddlewheeler like the DELTA QUEEN still excites the river dweller, so that its arrival is announced days in advance and the levee is lined with sightseers as it makes its landing. Brooding in the July sun while the passengers tour the countryside, the old dowager can still stir desire more unsettling than the workaday vessels a tenth of her age.

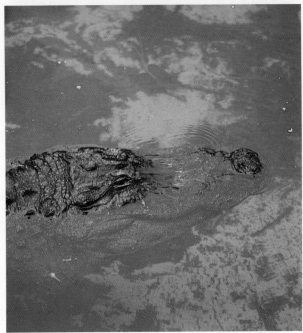

And the river bank children live amid beauties that will haunt their dreams if they drift away in later years.

37

Never finished because of the diversion of sensible work into the great stupidity of war, Longwood at Natchez has long been scoffed at by the architecturally orthodox as a folly. But a brief visit to the interior shows the designer was a man of innovative genius. More to the conventional taste is the feminine nestbuilding in the Victorian mode at The Burn.

Varina Howell married Jefferson Davis at the Briars which stands on a bluff with a magnificent view of a sweep of the river. With his own early manhood passed on the river in Vicksburg and his wife's youth spent within sight of its water, it is doubly puzzling why Davis let the river fall into Union hands and thus condemned the Confederacy to defeat.

During the brief glory of the Natchez plantation culture, the country's lords had such exquisite taste that even their outbuildings, like this structure beside the Briars, show more charm than all but a pitifully few modern buildings.

41

Largely tamed now, the big river still covets the great plain it once roamed freely. The floods that once plagued all the riverine lowlands have now been confined to a few square miles in the Lower Delta and even there decades pass before the river tries to reclaim its lost empire. But out of long habit, when the river dweller rises on a spring morning with the mists swirling low and the air smelling of rain, he checks the river gauge, feeling a little foolish for worrying about a long dead threat but feeling a little better if the crest has passed for this year.

CHAPTER 3

Faulkner Haunted Country

ALONG THE TENNESSEE BORDER, the middle counties of Mississippi work at being stereotypes of magnolia-scented Old Dixie. They get help from their steamy history which lends horror, glamour and fascination to gothic romances of the Old South, especially in the works of the region's greatest son, William Faulkner.

On the moonlight and magnolias side of north Mississippi, Holly Springs sprang into existence in 1832 immediately after the Chickasaw Indians were run out of the country. Skipping the log cabin phase of frontier living, early immigrants from the First Families of Virginia built colonnaded copies of the home manse. Many of them still stand as witnesses to the grand but stuffy taste of the well-born settlers.

Before even the first planter chopped down the first hickory tree and thrust the first cotton seed into the soil, the first arrival was almost certainly a shirt tail lawyer drawn by the promise of profitable wrangling over metes and bounds in the newly-platted country. Only a year after incorporation, Holly Springs had fourteen law offices, staffed mostly by self-educated or, more likely, uneducated frontier barristers. In the words of one of their own, they had come to enrich themselves with ". . . magnificent operations in the land offices! . . . in Indian Affairs—swindling Indians by the nation! Stealing their land by the township!"

During the Civil War, the town suffered so many raids by both armies —sixty-one altogether—that friendships and loyalties became hopelessly confused. At one mansion, legend has it that the grateful mistress of the household hid a Union officer from Confederate raiders because the Yankee had kept his own people from thrusting a hospital on her hospitality.

At the next mansion, the story is that General Grant's wife was surprised there by a Confederate raid and saved her husband's papers from nosy intelligence officers by persuading the chivalrous Southern commander to respect the privacy of her boudoir. When Grant retook the town,

Revealing a startling familiarity with the legendry of his home county, an Oxford youngster obligingly strikes the pose of Benjy behind the very fence that probably inspired William Faulkner's THE SOUND AND THE FURY. He is growing up against a backdrop that has become world famed as the scene of the Nobel Laureate's gothic fables. Many of Faulkner's contemporaries knew little of his great art, but the young people know.

he returned the courtesy—and was equally gulled—by ordering his troops to stay a block away from the place, thus unwittingly setting up a safe house for relays of Rebel spies.

The flush times were great while they lasted, and the ladies of Holly Springs each spring go into a frenzy of housekeeping preparing for the annual pilgrimage which glorifies those distant days. Though their husbands laud progress and the New South at the chicken-and-green-pea luncheons of their civic clubs, the hostesses of Holly Springs sternly remain true to hoop skirts and crinolines, at least for the duration of the hoped-for influx of tourists. The shrewd ladies are mining the architectural riches left behind by the planters as single-mindedly as their ancestors mined the land.

Hard times honed those survival skills all over the northern tier, as any city slicker will discover if he trades at the flea market of Ripley on the first Monday of every month.

To a writer like me who considers William Faulkner the greatest author America has produced, outperforming even Twain and clearly outclassing Hemingway, Ripley is something of a shrine. It was the home of the Nobel Laureate's great-grandfather, Colonel William Faulkner, the first writer of the family and transparently the model for the Colonel Sartoris who brought aristocratic dash and cavalier violence to the Yoknapatawpha saga.

The story of the elder Faulkner's life is an almost uninterrupted series of armed street brawls in the frontier fashion. During peacetime, the diminutive game cock shot and stabbed his neighbors wholesale in impromptu duels that seemed to be a common street entertainment of the day. In war, he raised two cavalry regiments to harry the Northern foe, first at Manassas and then as one of Nathan Bedford Forrest's irregular cavalry.

Col. Faulkner's adventures as a frontier swashbuckler and guerilla chieftain inspired great stretches of the Yoknapatawpha legend and are retold more or less as they happened by his great-grandson. But what truly gripped the younger Faulkner's imagination was the old man's novel *The White Rose of Memphis*, a runaway best seller in its time and lively reading to this day. From the time he was a schoolboy, young William told anybody who was curious that he was going to grow up "to be a writer like my great-granddaddy."

Col. Faulkner (he was born with the "u" but later pared the name to a more compact Falkner) was shot down by a former friend.

Over the murdered colonel's grave in Ripley's cemetery stands the old man's statue, a monument he commissioned during his sole voyage to the Old World. It is significant that he chose to be carved in eternal stone not as a duelist or cavalry officer armed with colt and saber, but as an intellectual with a stack of heavy books propped against his calf.

A few miles east lies Brice's Crossroads, a rural woods and pastureland humming with bees under the Mississippi sun, as drowsily peaceful a landscape as the state affords. But in 1864 as the war was winding down, Colonel Faulkner's outfit, led by the untutored military genius Forrest, ambushed a Union column there and soaked the roads and bridges with blood.

Bewitched by the romance of their ancestral home country, the belles of the border counties happily don the gowns of their great grandmothers and play at being Scarlett for a day. The role becomes big business during the Pilgrimages that show off antebellum homes like this one at Holly Springs.

Faulkner has left his stamp everywhere in Yokna-patawpha County. His old farm is still intact, though its biggest crop today is probably covies of wild quail sporting through the protective brush. Beside a country road the motorist passes a ram-shackle country store without knowing it was the model for Varner's store in THE HAMLET. But most of the literary world recognizes at a glance the stately facade of Rowan Oak where Faulkner wrote most of his later works.

Commanded by one of the boneheads that the Union forces persisted in elevating to high office, the Federals marched under the blistering Mississippi summer sky clad in woolen winter uniforms. Forrest nicely calculated the point of their trek where they would be most sweatily exhausted but still short of collapsing for a restful bivouac. He dismounted his men and posted them deep in the tangled brush on each side of the road.

Supposedly superior in firepower because of Northern industrial might, the Union soldiers marched into battle with antiquated single-shot muskets. The Southern rustic and slave trader Forrest had bought from his own pocket 500 long-barreled six-shooters, the invention of the Yankee genius Samuel Colt. Forrest's country boys used the latest and most murderous tool of Northern technology to pour fire into the weary enemy. The Union column was sent reeling back down the road to Ripley with staggering losses.

Looping back westward, the road runs by the Ackia Battlefield where centuries ago the Chickasaws, with the help of a few English traders, defeated a mixed force of French and Choctaws. Legend reports that a priest refused to allow his captors to turn him free but insisted on joining the other French prisoners at the stake, thus raising the ticklish ethical question—did he show a salvationworthy zeal for martyrdom or did he commit the unforgivable sin of despair by committing suicide? In any case, it was an act of looney heroics well suited to the mythical countryside that surrounds Oxford, made world famous by Faulkner as Yoknapatawpha County.

The very earth of a great writer's homeland, its dialect, local tall tales, manners and jealousies, its small bigotries and large sins inevitably infuse the work of a great regional writer. But no writer so consciously used his homeland to great effect as William Faulkner, the "owner and sole proprietor" of Yoknapatawpha County.

The landscape of that dreamland won Faulkner a Nobel Prize in 1949. More important, it won him a place among the giants of the earth for all time. Though the true map of that mythical countryside existed only in his handsome head, Lafayette County with its environs is the material from which he fashioned his mirror image of reality.

The courthouse in Oxford—the very navel of Yoknapatawpha County—remains unchanged since its rebuilding after Yankee soldiers burned it in 1864. Still it dominates the square, "quadrangular around it, the stores, two-storey, the offices of the lawyers and doctors and dentists, the lodge-rooms and auditoriums above them; . . . the four broad diverging avenues straight as plumb-lines in the four directions, becoming the network of roads and by-roads until the whole county would be covered with it. . . ."

In pursuit of Yoknapatawpha, I begin my nostalgic trip at the courthouse square, for Faulkner himself measured Yoknapatawpha distances from this zero point.

Old-timers sit around the courthouse lawn telling ancient lies at glacial speed, drawing them out so that they will last till sunset has ended their daily duty of watching over Oxford's downtown affairs.

"Yep, I knew him right well," says one old fellow, neatly clad in shiny black jacket and crisp starched white shirt, buttoned at the throat but tieless in the currently fashionable mode of his set—by "currently" I mean, of course, for the last one hundred years.

"Used to come around to sit with us and watch the doings around the square, but never said much. Kind of a strange quiet one, he was." And then, to explain Faulkner's peculiarities, he adds, "He wrote a book, you know."

On the south side of the courthouse lawn, atop his column with his back turned disdainfully on the north, stands the mandatory Confederate soldier, the one that the halfwit Benjy in *The Sound and the Fury* insisted on passing to his left or he would set up a nerve-shattering wail. Today, the Oxford Police Department has declared the streets around the square one-way so that everybody, like Benjy, must pass the statue to his left, regardless of his own neurotic compulsions.

Using the homely materials of his own county, Faulkner built a mythical empire called Yoknapatawpha. The monument to the Lost Cause at the courthouse square, the yeomanry of the hills about the town, the wily strategems of the domino duelists in the downtown park furnished his genius the makings of a gothic epic.

To visit the presumed real life originals of Yoknapatawpha's scenes, I circle the square and head westward, passing on the left an outside stairway that leads to second-story offices that Hollywood filmed as the chambers of the gabby lawyer Gavin Stephens in the movie *Intruder in the Dust.* Across the street is a small red brick building with a bizarre bay window. It once was the seat of lawyer Phil Stone, the probable model for Gavin Stephens.

Looping left and returning to the square on Van Buren Street, on the right is an empty shell that was the Lyric Theater which for a brief night was the center of the entertainment world as it presented the premiere of *Intruder in the Dust.* In the same cavernous husk, Faulkner's father Murray long ago ran a livery stable.

Running southward from the square, Lamar Avenue is one of those "four broad diverging avenues straight as plumb-lines" that Faulkner laid out in his "Courthouse" section of *Requiem for a Nun*. By turning left on Buchanan to Thirteenth Street, I find half-hidden behind rank shrubbery the Edwin Chandler house, generally accepted by scholars as the model for the Compson mansion in *The Sound and the Fury*.

On the west side of Lamar and a short distance south, I walk up the rutted gravel road to Rowan Oak, Faulkner's last home. As administrator of the grounds, the University of Mississippi maintains Rowan Oak as nearly as possible the way it looked the day he died.

The interior has the fusty elegance that befitted a Depression era rustic nabob. The main interest lies in his workroom with its battered old manual typewriter and the skeleton outline for Holy Week, as developed in *A Fable*, sketched by Magic Marker in Faulkner's hand on the walls. Apparently even the creator of that tangled epic could not follow the action without a road map.

I turn toward the Ole Miss campus where Faulkner was once a special student—though he had never graduated from high school—and later a postmaster. He was not a success in either role.

Just inside the campus gates stands another Confederate soldier, a statue originally destined for the courthouse lawn but somehow diverted to the university grounds. Faulkner's grandmother Sally was outraged by the move and badgered the town fathers till they put up another statue on the square.

On the university library's third floor is the Mississippi Collection, including his Nobel Prize, and on the outside wall of the building, in raised metal letters, are the concluding words of his Nobel speech asserting that "Man will not merely endure, he will prevail."

To get to the real heart of the rustic country from which sprang the peasantry that inhabit the underworld of Yoknapatawpha, I drive south of town on the Old Taylor Road. The mixed pine and hardwood scrub forest, the gullies eroded into the red clay hillsides formed the backwoods country that disgorged into

An old pensioner recalls without undue excitement or reverence his friendship with the great writer, recounting mildly scandalous anecdotes about youthful escapades together. Visitors from foreign lands, however, study the layout of the house and gardens of any spot reported to have been used by Faulkner as a model. Even the scribblings the writer put on his workshop wall to guide him through A FABLE are preserved as carefully as one of Buddha's teeth in Ceylon.

53

I DECLINE TO ACCEPT THE END OF MAN...
I BELIEVE THAT MAN WILL NOT MERELY
ENDURE: HE WILL PREVAIL.

WILLIAM FAULKNER

Faulkner's tales the brutish Bundren family of *As I Lay Dying* and the snake-sly Flem Snopes who undermined by guile and greed the old aristocracy of Yoknapatawpha society.

Faulkner wrote of universal pains and passions—lust, treachery, courage, honor, despair—and so he is understood by everybody, at least in the soaring lucid stretches of his sometimes tangled works. But the reader who travels over the earth his hill folk tilled, who scratches the goats in the dooryards of hill cabins and shivers in the musty cool of decaying mansions, that reader rereads Faulkner's myth with a new feeling of sympathy and pity—even distant kinship with the joyless but sometimes preposterously funny peasantry and the doomed aristocracy of Yoknapatawpha County.

From the doughty little colonel who fought with Bedford Forrest to stymie a far more powerful enemy to the writer who won worldwide fame after decades of discouragement, the Faulkners have shown a hard-headed stubbornness and dash that make up one of the many forms of courage.

G W WALLACE

CO G
14 TEX INF
CSA

The Hustling East

E<small>AST</small> OF YOKNAPATAWPHA, a block of counties, running from Tennessee down the Alabama line, spends less time looking toward the myth-haunted past and more toward the fabled future. The cavalier and Southern comfort past of Yoknapatawpha was made of saddles and sabers, of Southern fried grits and turnip greens; the computer and fast-food future of the Alabama border counties will be made of bytes and pizzas.

Just a few days after he had routed a powerful Yankee column at Brice's Crossroads, Forrest got a rare comeuppance at Tupelo where Union forces first drove him off, but then retreated, possibly appalled by their effrontery in dealing the Confederate genius an unaccustomed defeat. A National Battlefield Park now commemorates the affair.

Though such a dashing encounter elsewhere in the South would excite annual flag-raising ceremonies and hoop-skirted Confederate Balls, in Tupelo local civic leaders give the tussle little thought and busy themselves instead with a science-fiction tomorrow.

Guided by pocketbook pragmatism and an eminently sensible and civic-minded newspaperman, Tupelo's leaders have studied and made terms with the probable shape of the twenty-first century. They are preparing the citizenry for that future, unsettling though it may appear in its dependence on discomfortingly smart computers running frighteningly mindless robots.

As the basic step toward preparing for future technology of bizzare complexity, George McLean, publisher of the *Daily Journal*, has underwritten a supplementary teaching program to boost reading skills of Lee County's rural first graders.

"Reading is the most basic of skills, and children who are poor readers in the first grade are poor readers forever," Mr. McLean said.

Holding up a copy of his daily, he pronounced the kind of hard-nosed truth that is changing the face of the ten northeastern counties.

While the cannons were still echoing, the kindly ladies of Columbus showed the world a touching example of the art of healing by decorating the graves not only of their fallen Southern heroes but also of the Northern dead. Their generous gesture fittingly became the first Memorial Day.

In the northeast counties around Tupelo, an enlightened leadership has determined that the youngsters will go into the next century fully armed with sound education. A reading program begun on the first day of school has boosted achievement scores. More importantly, it has made reading skills as prestigious for playground status as mighty muscles. Paying for it all will be the farmer who has been persuaded to switch from trying to row crop his exhausted land to raising hogs with the help of science.

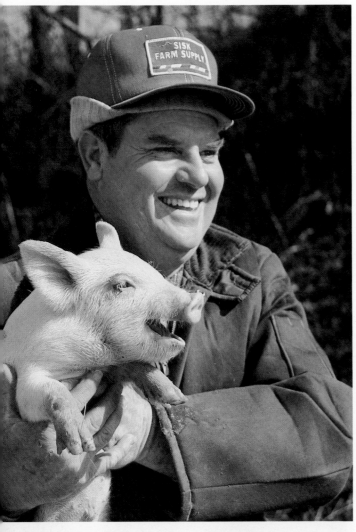

"If they can't read around here, my newspaper is out of business—and so is every other enterprise. You can't master even the simplest subject from the snippets of information offered on television. You sure can't master the formidable technology that the next decade is going to throw at us if you can understand only what flickers briefly on a television screen.

"If every community put as much money and effort into hard education as it does into football," George said, "we wouldn't be worried about falling behind other advanced nations in technology."

The reading program in English is only the beginning of training planned for Tupelo's youth by the Community Development Foundation. The foundation's Harry Martin showed us a program for making the area's schoolchildren literate in a weird new literature by teaching them the several arcane languages that computers speak. The young hopefuls will study electronic data processing from the early grades through graduation, so that a computer keyboard will be as familiar a teaching aid to them as chalk and a blackboard.

Pursuing a plan reminiscent of the Japanese system, counselors are training themselves to help children find a career slot they can slip into during childhood and move through till they join the next generation's industrial workforce. In the vocational workshops, we found the youngsters punching keyboards that instructed robotlike machines to punch, slice, perforate, bend, twist, drill, and crunch material into desired shapes.

"We're the first community in the TVA region to teach our kids the new skill of robotics," Harry Martin said. "They've got to be able to run those keyboards to survive in the age that's coming.

"Being a farmer won't help to escape the demands of the new technological age," Martin said.

"Farmers used to think their job was five months of brutal back labor followed by seven months of hunting and fishing, but that's a quick trip to the poorhouse today. Farmers have to spend twelve months putting high technology to work boosting production, or they go broke."

In 1955, Lee County had 5,900 farmers. In the 1980 census, it had lost all but 487 farmers to the boll weevil and competition from the vast operations of agribusiness corporations in the lowlands.

"In these hills, we can't compete with the huge Delta plantations in growing cotton and other row crops," Martin said, "but we can grow chickens and hogs as well as anybody."

Two immense packing plants at Tupelo and Water Valley were killing an impressive 8,500 hogs daily—most of them imported from everywhere in the South except Northeast Mississippi—when the foundation began urging the region's remaining farmers to provide the porkers.

"Importing hogs is like importing oil," said Martin. "We're going to stop that bleeding away of income that belongs to us. First, we are growing grain to feed hogs for the first profit, and then we are feeding the grain to our own hogs for the second profit. If we raise half the present slaughter from our own animals, that will mean $200 million annually to the region. Turn that money over four or five times, as it does normally, and you have almost a trillion dollars of new money injected into the region's purse."

Despite the concentration of northeast Mississippi's leaders on the technology of the future, Tupelo's most famous son by far was an artist. The humble cottage where Elvis Presley was born is preserved as a shrine visited yearly by thousands who marvel at the simple origins of a Mississippi lad who parleyed Apollonian

A valiant band of pioneers makes astonishingly drinkable wines from the native muscadine grape and the state university viticulture lab pursues an elusive hybrid that will have the quality of California with the hardiness of Mississippi. Meanwhile, the common man consumes by the gallon the old Southern comfort of iced tea. The cafe tries to jazz up its image by serving it in a container that offered white lightning in a ruder day.

good looks and a throbbing baritone into a fortune that rivalled an oil sheik's.

Elsewhere along the Alabama border, local leaders also have a slightly disturbing intensity about attracting more turret lathes to replace the spinning wheels of the past. A few of the border towns have no apologies to make to other historic sites, however, for their nurture of antebellum structures.

Aberdeen, for instance, is chock-a-block with beautiful old mansions in splendid repair. Even better, some brilliant local thinker has persuaded merchants to shelter entire blocks of their downtown sidewalks under old-fashioned flat roofs supported by curbside pillars in a charming revival of the eminently sensible architectural fashion of the nineteenth-century South.

Certainly Columbus has few apologies to make for its historic preservation. Besides the professionally historic mansion Waverley, the town has thirty-eight delightful old places on its driving tour and another couple of dozen other restorations not formally listed.

At Friendship Cemetery, almost before the cannons stopped rumbling, the local ladies began the healing process by decorating the graves of Confederate and Union soldiers, a custom that became nationwide and is still observed as Memorial Day. The Union bodies were later moved, but in the cemetery there still lie the fallen Confederates.

A far livelier scene is the campus of the Mississippi University for Women, popularly known as The W

Along the Alabama border lie some improbable sights—a waterfall tumbling over rocky terraces, U.S. Navy airmen training for carrier flights, and a humble cottage that sheltered the birth of a lad destined to become a singer worshipped by millions in corners of the earth that have never heard the name of Caruso or Pavarotti. Elvis Presley left Tupelo to make it very big indeed in the large world.

and the oldest state college for women in the United States. The pride of The W's faculty is the home economics department; the most prestigious extracurricular activity is the modeling squad for showing off campus-designed apparel.

At Starkville, just twenty-two miles east, the engineering and architectural student's principal fashion accessory is an electronic calculator. At the veterinarian college, the mode is for jackets and ties for the young gentlemen, equivalently sober garb for the young ladies. Anybody wandering the college's corridors in farm style jeans has strayed from a more fashion conscious quarter. The students have little time for sartorial concerns, for hours are grindingly long.

"Analysis has shown that a veterinarian must learn 10,000 facts and skills," according to Dean James Miller. "That works out to a fact or a skill every 20 minutes during the entire course."

During my visit to the labyrinthine 375,000-square-foot building that houses the veterinarian school, I was struck by the high percentage of girl students—about 40 percent usually—who attack the gruelling schedule with no more apparent physical or mental fatigue than their male colleagues. And no more of them are attracted to the cute little lap pet trade than the hairy-chested man.

In the more genial setting of a Tudor style baronial hall with chemical labs and bottling plants cunningly hidden behind a nineteenth century decor, Dr. Boris Stejanovic pursued the pleasant goal of the ultimate wine from Mississippi-grown grapes. Against a backdrop of panelling and sporting prints, the portly and good-natured wine master told of his lifelong fascination with the grape.

"When I was a boy in Yugoslavia, I helped my father make millions of liters of wine," he said, "but the only technology they had over there was elbow grease, so I came over to find an easier way."

He came to Mississippi as a soil microbiologist, and in 1974 turned to the task of producing elbow grease-less wine in the Department of Enology and Viticulture.

"So far, no vine succeeds so well in Mississippi as the native muscadine," he said. "Diseases get the vinifera vines of Europe and California. We are testing one hundred grape varieties, including many hybrid mixtures of muscadine and French vinifera, and they are looking good. But pure muscadine is still the grape for Mississippi."

Down the road a few miles at Thousand Oaks Winery, I interrupted young William Burgin at a taste-testing of his product. Warily, I sipped a white wine made from the Magnolia variety of muscadines. To my pleased surprise, William's muscadines made a pleasant aperitif wine.

In European style, the harvest at Thousand Oaks is a campout and lawn party for amateur pickers seeking to be farmers for a day. Between July and October, groups of forty or so from Atlanta, Jackson, New Orleans, and half a dozen schools drive in to gather the ripened fruit and pass it to the crushers a ton at a time. Lunch is on the house, of course, and so is whatever vintage the gourmet picker imagines will go best with a salami and kosher dill sandwich. Under the sweltering sun, most pickers stick with a good, if not a great, beer.

In 1961 the United States Navy most improbably plunked down an aviation training base at Meridian, far from the sea. The navy jet has become to Meridian what the seagoing ship-of-the-line has long been to Norfolk, Virginia—a welcome stabilizer during the economy's rollercoaster ups and downs. After the nervous straining to catch up with an onrushing tomorrow I found along the northern stretches of the Alabama border, Meridian seemed a pleasant hideout for people, content with a comfortable today.

Their countryside encourages insouciance. Stony outcroppings, steep river banks, dense woods make the lands around the Chunky River look more like the approaches to the Rockies than the piney woods border of a cotton state. Rounding a curve in the Chunky River in a canoe, I was startled to come upon Dunn's Falls, a cascade with a fifty-foot drop that would excite grateful comment in Colorado.

The folk of Meridian may know what they are doing in not striving to have a paper mill built on the pretty little river.

This Piney Woods country is no place to look for the antebellum palaces that grace the Northern border towns. Before the Civil War, most of the area was a vast forest of yellow pine with rare clearings where small farmers struggled, barely beyond the stage of frontier scrabbling for survival.

During the lumber boom around the turn of the century, Laurel sprang into existence as a sawmill town. Even from the beginning, a strange ferment stirred Laurel. The WPA Guide to the state notes that the early sawmill hands spent their first paychecks on secondhand pianos.

Less wonder, then, that the greatest operatic voice of this century came from this sawmill town lost in the Piney Woods. When Leontyne Price made her New York debut in *Il Trovatore*, she lifted the audience out of their seats in an explosion of astonished joy. Her triumph brought great pride but little surprise to opera lovers in her home state, for she had toured there as a nineteen-year-old student, singing trial concerts accompanied by her mentor, Mrs. Alexander Chisholm of Laurel.

Half of her audiences came only to see the spectacle, astonishing in that time, of a high-born white woman taking second place to a black girl. That magic voice stunned them all, true music lovers and curiosity seekers, so that her subsequent career, probably more triumphant than any since Caruso's, comes as no surprise to her fellow Mississippians, who are universally happy to see one of us making it in the big time.

It is a little odd that Laurel's most famous citizen should be black, however, for Laurel is in a pocket of almost pure white history. Its home county of Jones had few slaveholders.

The men of Jones, who worked their poor farms

If you are a Southern girl, you can't resist putting a bit of dash into the local uniform. For the price of a few feathers, you can lift yourself to the level of a trend setter in junior circles.

For a few days every summer, all of Mississippi holds a homecoming at the Neshoba County Fair. Entire families move in for the duration, swapping gossip, risking a buck or two on the ponies or acting out romantic fantasies, as appropriate to the generations.

Already a veteran of the fair scene, she hoards a souvenir that won a valued prize for her clan in the tribal gathering of rural Mississippians.

home grounds and did not die at distant Chancellorsville or Gettysburg for a cause they had come to detest.

For what is essentially a sawmill town, Hattiesburg probably has the smartest looking downtown pedestrians of any industrial small city in the South. Though the conversion of pine trees into building materials keeps the city going, the most visible industry is the conversion of raw youngsters into college-trained sophisticates. They make a decorative street scene.

Anybody pursuing any theatrical enterprise in the big show centers soon begins to bump into graduates from the University of Southern Mississippi—set designers, lighting technicians, cameramen, actors, wardrobe designers. The American Rose Society garden on the 940-acre campus, the great collection of children's book manuscripts and pictures at the library, and the Natural History Museum have their charms, but most visitors wind up watching the hustling students at the Performing Arts Center.

An appeal to a coarser clientele backed the big fight at Purvis in 1889. Jake Kilrain and John L. Sullivan, the Boston Strong Boy, had been run out of New Orleans as sinners—no mean feat when you come to think of it—and were forced to put on the epic struggle for the bare-knuckle heavyweight championship of the world in a yellow pine glade. The brave lads had been training among the worldly pleasures of the Creole capital and were not in tiptop shape. In the forty-fourth round, Jake Kilrain sportingly withheld his onslaught while John L. was throwing up.

"I never strike a man while he is vomiting," Kilrain explained grandly, thus adding a hitherto unthought-of-codicil to the Gentleman's Code of Honor.

He paid dearly for his gesture, for his second had to throw in the towel in the seventy-fifth round, ending history's last championship bare-knuckle fight. Disgusted spectators agreed that the fight at Purvis is probably what killed the sport.

Just south is Stone County, distinguished in Mississippi history by being the only county that never harbored a slave.

Somewhere south of Stone County's seat at Wiggins you smell the exciting salt tang of the sea, for the Gulf of Mexico and Mississippi's delightful mini-coast is just over the next hill or so.

with their own calloused hands, refused to die for wealthy landowners who sent regiments of blacks to work their cottonfields. When the Confederacy sent cavalry to round them up as deserters, they slipped into the woods, proclaimed the Free State of Jones, and gave the organized military an advanced taste of Vietnam. Loading their double-barreled shotguns with a handful of musketballs in each barrel, they mowed down their pursuers from almost arm's length in woodland ambushes. Their captain Newton Knight gets a mixed press from modern historians. Some call him a great libertarian and guerilla genius; others call him a rascally bandit. In any case, his men fought on their

CHAPTER 5

The Gulf Coast

MISSISSIPPIANS HAVE A TALENT for sinking
their lives, their fortunes, and their sacred honor
in Lost Causes, so that the state's history begins appropriately
at Pascagoula on the Singing River, for there a legend tells of
a superbly looney Lost Cause, worthy of Mississippi. The local tribe,
having been defeated by neighboring barbarians, supposedly escaped from
redskin carpetbagger rule by joining hands, striking up a community sing-
along, and sinking together to their deaths in the sluggish river, their
breathing impeded but their honor intact. Romantics insist you can still
hear the suicidal braves humming below the water, hence the Singing River
business.

Local legends on this coast all seem to have to do with water. Between
the soup-warm Gulf and the marshy backwoods the people are pressed into a narrow strip of dry land along the coast. Dark bayous snake across
the country. Each pond and stream has its story and, in keeping with the
unwritten instructions for constructing a Southern legend, it's usually a
gloomy one.

Consider a brackish lake a short walk west of Pascagoula. Near it is the
childhood home of the Union Admiral David Farragut, who was reared as
far south as you can go in Mississippi but who led a Yankee fleet into the
Gulf of Mexico to blockade his home coast and starve his former neighbors. Why? Because he was loyal to his oath as an American naval officer
to uphold the Constitution of the United States?

"Nonsense," says the Gulf Coast legend maven.

"Loyalty! Not from that renegade. Around here we know what really
happened. When David was young, he fooled around with a helpless or-
phan girl who had been entrusted to his folks, and when he got her in
trouble, he just ran off and left her to face the music which wasn't going
to be the wedding march. She did the only decent thing and drowned her-
self in that pool yonder, poor thing, but not before she put a curse on the

land and on young David. That's why he went with the Yankees and that's why his land has never prospered."

It was a small bore curse of short range, for just a pistol ball's carry westward the living is easy. The coastal marshes shrink and disappear, the resin-bearing pines and the dollar-bearing tourists come down to the white sand beach.

On the site of Old Biloxi (now Ocean Springs) where in 1699 the Sieur d'Iberville and a shipload of Frenchmen established the first permanent settlement in the Mississippi Valley, the Indians smeared themselves with white clay to honor the first white men they had ever seen. Today, paleface tourists from the North smear themselves with oil and lie in the sun to turn their skins Indian red.

Offshore, a stubble of pinetops frets the sky, and on a clear day you can see the low-lying silhouette of the barrier islands, most of them protected in the Gulf Islands National Seashore. The strip of water between, known as Mississippi Sound, is shallow, tepid, and muddy, so every invader of this coast has anchored off Ship Island and sent men and supplies ashore by shallow boat.

The French first landed there before moving ashore. A short time later, a Spanish governor sailed with a flotilla to drive off the French but was shipwrecked and committed the socially awkward gaffe of submitting to rescue by the enemy he had come to massacre.

The nun-chaperoned maidens "of impeccable background" who 250 years ago landed on this island, *casquettes* or hope chests in hand, were the first white women in the Mississippi Valley. They had been sent out by the home government as prospective wives for the womenless French settlers who had developed a deplorable tendency to fritter away their time chasing Indian girls instead of working up a sweat building colonial fortunes for the greater glory of the French court. One of the reverend chaperones wrote home that all the girls quickly found suitable husbands.

As part of the War of 1812, a luckless flotilla of sixty British warships based their campaign against New Orleans on Ship Island. Reeling back from the rude reception given them at Chalmette by Andrew Jackson's backwoods sharpshooters and the cannoneers of the freebooter Jean Lafitte, the British packed their

Once the Gulf of Mexico covered one-fifth of present Mississippi and reached beyond Memphis. Only yesterday in geologic time, the big river dropped enough silt to drive the gulf southward to its present bed. Seen from the old continental cape north of Jackson, the old seabed now grows vast forests and farm crops.

dead commander, Sir Edward Packenham, into a barrel of rum to keep him for the long voyage home.

Fort Massachusetts that now stands on Ship Island was built by order of Jefferson Davis, of all people, when he was secretary of the army for the nation he later repudiated. It was held by Union forces almost from the beginning of the Civil War and was the base for Admiral Farragut's assault on the Mississippi River that was far more successful than the British raid before him.

Today, like an immense funnel, the Mississippi River Basin drains hundreds of thousands of tourists from almost half the United States and parts of Canada and deposits them on fifty miles of beach and golf course, resort hotel and luxurious restaurant, park and garden along the Mississippi shore.

In summer, tourists flock from the Southern states to escape hometown heat under the Gulf beach breezes. In winter, visitors flee the Arctic blasts of Northern states to golf in a climate kept mild by the great shallow tub of warm water just offshore. In early spring, when snows still cover Northern flower beds, the coast is an unbroken azalea garden blooming under enormous moss-hung live oaks. In the fall, fishing in the Gulf or the brackish waters inland lures tens of thousands of anglers from distant and less densely populated waters —populated with fish, that is.

Known to regular visitors simply as "the Coast," the Mississippi playground stretches about fifty miles westward through Biloxi and Gulfport to peter out in coastal marshes somewhere around Waveland on the road to New Orleans.

Before the mid-1950s, the Mississippi coast had been a popular resort, but its beach had never been impressive—too shallow and muddy. Nevertheless, the citizenry was horrified when the United States Army Corps of Engineers dredged tons of black spoil onto the shore. With the first rain, however, whatever it was that made the muck black leached out, leaving crystalline sand as white as sugar along the longest manmade beach in the world.

An environmental experiment on Mississippi's Gulf Coast, begun only in 1974 and involving only the nesting habits of a minor flock of shore birds, may change the face of that tourist-oriented region, may thwart the fury of tropical storms, and may serve as a clinic and classroom to teach tens of thousands the exquisitely sensitive relationships between man and his world in the web of life.

Conscious of the dollar value of the artificial sandy slope into the Gulf's warm waters, county authorities maintain a patrol of machine sweepers and bulldozers that keep the beach clean and push the sand from the sea wall back toward the water after high winds and tides. Everybody admires the service and the flawless stretch of unblemished sugar-sand.

When dredges cast tons of ugly black muck on the coastal beach, residents thought the tourist trade had been demolished. The first hard rain leached out the spoil and left miles of sugar-white beach that now supports games, nesting wildlife and the tidal creatures that inspire the artist.

Neil Ballard works at Ocean Springs at the almost forgotten art of pewter work. Judy Toups is the acknowledged Bird Lady of the Gulf Coast, the champion of all oppressed feathered species.

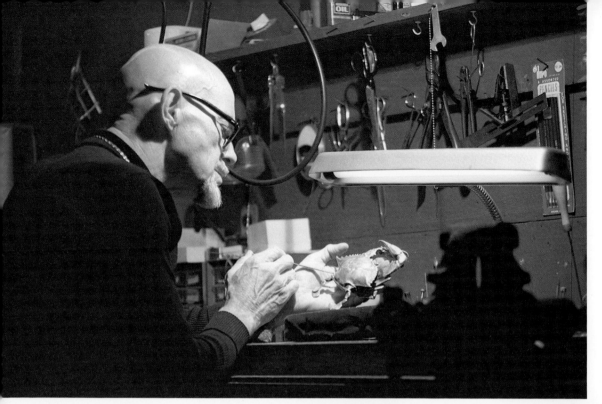

We have here a remarkable sequence showing the beginnings and completion of a masterwork that apparently consumed the entire childhood of the artists.

Everybody goes down to the sea to live off the poor fish, from black skimmer to Memphis tycoon.

81

Except the bird lovers.

"Back to the dawn of time, least terns by the thousands have come from Central and South America to scoop out nests in the sand," said Judy Toups, one of the Gulf Coast bird ladies who ferociously guard their feathered charges. "They came to the beach in May, their hatchlings pipped in June, and by July the whole family could fly. The peaceloving birds had a good thing here because the area has few predatory birds to rob their nests.

"Then along came the sweeping machines. They chugged down the beach every night sucking up nests, eggs, fledglings, and brooding adults along with the pop bottles and beer cans. By 1973 the nesting colony was down to twenty pairs, and they could have disappeared on any given night."

The birders of the Coast bombarded the county board of supervisors with requests to leave unswept at least part of the beach as a nesting refuge. Public opposition to the refuge was immediate and mostly virulent, especially from hotel owners along the beach.

The county supervisors finally were persuaded to pick out a one-mile stretch where there somehow happened to be no hotels, a rare occurence on that coast. There, they put up warning signs and ordered beach crews to clean only by hand.

As though they had received a cable, the terns got the word somehow in far-off South America and came back instantly and in throngs. Within a year, a thousand pairs nested, and now late arrivals crowded out of the refuge are setting up their satellite rookeries.

An unexpected reaction that probably saved the refuge came from the unpredictable public itself. Far from being offended by being excluded from the beach to favor a passel of birds, they flock to the refuge. During nesting season, visitors show a ferocious protectiveness for the birds. They erect barriers of twigs around nests to keep the big feet of other visitors from crushing the eggs. While one expert was handling a tern for banding, a passing truck driver bellowed, "You put down that there little old bird, lady, before you hurt it."

Nature immediately began to show that every environmental action has astonishing side effects. The unswept beach pushed up sea grasses and shore plants in startling contrast to the pure sand surface elsewhere.

"It looks like a cow pasture," one letter complained. "When are you going to bale the hay?"

Today's youngsters will never know the joy of snitching a chunk of ice from the back of a wagon while the driver tolerantly pretended he did not know he was being hijacked. A store-bought snow cone just doesn't have the same zing.

Others thoughtfully noted the dunelets building up about the grass clumps, the sharp reduction of blowing of the fine sand.

"It costs $300,000 a year to clear sand off the highway," a road foreman said. "Anything that will hold it down is to the good, including little birds." Most of the housewives along the beach agree.

Naturalists have long known the value of shore grasses and creepers for stabilizing sand beaches. The Gulf Coast Research Laboratory at Ocean Springs, a branch of the Mississippi system for higher education, maintains a special botanical section to work out the most effective methods of introducing shore plants to a threatened beach.

The laboratory's studies were spurred by the catastrophic hurricane Camille in 1969 which carried away vast stretches of unstabilized beach on the mainland. The beach had to be rebuilt a second time at great expense by dredging sand from the Gulf.

The barrier islands eight to twelve miles offshore suffered more permanent damage. The major attraction for visitors, Ship Island, was permanently cut in two. The two-mile cut across its middle has developed a deep channel scoured out by running currents, so Ship Island will probably never be rejoined. The island's Fort Massachusetts barely escaped being undercut by loss of the beach along its western wall. Since the storm, dredges have packed in sandy spoil taken from the channel, but the beach continued to erode eighteen feet a year. Because the island is part of the National Park Service's Gulf Islands National Seashore, federal officials authorized experiments by the laboratory.

Working under the direction of Dr. Lionel Eleuterius, head of the botany section, workmen put down sixty acres of bitter panicum plants on three-foot centers.

"We had one hundred percent survival," said Dr. Eleuterius. "The patches have grown together as a solid carpet in most places. Where the patches stand separate, they have built four-foot hummocks, a clear indication of their dune-building power. All this in one year.

"Since the panicum has anchored the sand, other plants, especially the beautiful sea oats, will move in quickly and the stabilizing dune-building process will proceed at full gallop. There is no doubt about what is happening. The grasses have won."

On Ship Island, Park Service Rangers guard the precious sea oats as they appear. At the entrance to the fort, a display case shows sprays of golden seed heads of sea oats with the warning:

"These sea oats play a vital role in stabilizing the sand on the barrier islands. Federal law prohibits the destruction or removal of these plants from National Seashores."

Within sight of the fort lies a terrible object lesson on the penalties of removing sea grasses. It is an open stretch of rolling sea where once stood Dog Island. A resort developer renamed it Caprice Island and built a hotel and pleasure palace. To kill two birds with one stone (an apt metaphor because many terns nested on the sandy island), he sold his crop of sea oats to a Chicago wholesale florist for use in dry arrangements, and he hired local women to clear the beach of grasses to make room for sunbathers.

Deprived of the network of sea oat roots, Caprice Island promptly blew away, hotel and all, leaving only the pipe from an artesian well projecting above the water to mark its grave. Recently, a shrimp boat tied up to the pipe in a storm and pulled it over, so nothing now marks the site of Dog Island where once the sea oats grew.

Ship Island is served in summer by two excursion boats from Biloxi and Gulfport and has a beach facing the Gulf, picnic tables, and guided tours of the fort from May through Labor Day. Rangers do not permit camping, however, to protect the fragile plantings. Campers have to move by private or chartered boat to the better-stabilized eastern half of the island or magnificently forested Horn Island still farther east.

There flourish American alligators, bald eagles, red cockaded woodpeckers, and ospreys, all endangered species elsewhere. Less endangered by a long sight are 200 feral hogs that have run wild for generations, raccoons that could prosper in Times Square, and otters. The park service boat captain, who took me to the island, gave an estimate of its rabbit population.

"Swing a club in the dark and you'll knock over three or four rabbits with the first lick."

Those barrier islands survive only because of the vegetation that has formed a precarious hold on the sands.

On the other two islands in the Mississippi District of the National Seashore, Horn and Petit Bois (pronounced "petty boy"), wildlife has evolved independently of the mainland. Wild mice, for instance, over the ages have paled to the color of the island sand. Alligators bask in ponds, rabbits hustle off through the grass, and the fattest raccoons I've ever seen waddle

The nearest thing to manna sent from heaven for the relief of the stricken of Mississippi during the Great Depression was the cottontail. Armed with a few batons cut from a pecan tree, hungry field hands tramped the countryside till they scared up a rabbit. A few potentates ostentatiously brought a shotgun to the hunt and even occasionally could afford a shell or two. But it was usually the strong-armed hurler of pecan bolts who brought down the quarry.

84

At Delta State students of the creative arts enjoy the heady experience of being respected as though they were living in Renaissance Florence.

about the woods at dusk. The two islands can be reached only by private boat; primitive camping is permitted.

There was a time when the Coast went into mothballs between Labor Day and Memorial Day. Then the Broadwater Beach Hotel at Biloxi acquired the Great Southern Golf Course beside the Gulf and in 1964 began to sell golfing packages to addicts in the upper Middle West. Now, twenty-two hotels offer golf packages. More than twenty thousand golfers come down each winter from Chicago alone.

Even more than the golf it is the water that lures most visitors.

Inland bayous and bays teem with freshwater fish. During low water, especially in autumn, fishermen catch with the same lures and in the same brackish waters salt and freshwater species. Sea trout are the commonest catch and make splendid eating, but the real prize is the redfish or channel bass, possibly the best eating of all the world's species. Most hotels will cook the guest's catch. A few will freeze it for shipment home.

Dozens of fishing camps rent boats, tackle, and bait and furnish guides to lead strangers through the tangle of inland waterways. A fleet of charter boats takes anglers far out to sea for deep-water sport fishing.

Whole families turn out at night when flounders come in to the beach front shallows. With a lantern and a gig, an ardent sportsman wading in knee-deep waters can spear up to fifty fish in a night. The best way to find out if the flounders are in is to look out the hotel window. If you see many bobbing lights on inshore waters, the locals have discovered the run and are harvesting.

From Mobile to Waveland there are nine yacht clubs, one for every ten miles. Each has the usual complement of power boats, but the coastal waters are ideal for sailing craft and so there is some kind of sailing regatta under way or being planned year round. (The prospect of winter sailing brings down some of the nation's top yachtsmen.)

The beach ends in coastal marsh just beyond Buccaneer State Park at Waveland. Just a short run down the interstate from the western end of the Gulf beach lies New Orleans. It is a sore temptation to run over for a gambol. If it is a Friday afternoon, however, you'll notice most of the traffic is going the other way as thousands of the Creole city's citizens flee toward the white sands and blue waters and green golf courses of the Gulf Coast.

They know a good thing when they see it.

On a spring Sunday the good Christian folk dress up for church; the little pagans go crawdadding in Rattlesnake Bayou.

Natchez and the Trace

REFILLING HIS KIT at the Natchez Boat Store before going back to work on a Mississippi River towboat, a young sailor dressed like an insurance salesman on a golfing vacation shook my belief that the river man was half-horse, half-alligator.

"Let me see," he mused, "hair oil . . . shaving lotion . . . hand cream . . . deodorant."

Hand cream, for Mike Fink's sake! The flatboatmen of the river's past had about as much use for creamy lotions on their hairy paws as a grizzly bear. Trying to picture a one-gallused Kaintuck patting on a deodorant floored my imagination.

River literature has universally painted those river men as hard-bitten brutes who floated a year's production of the Ohio Valley frontier to the world market at New Orleans, where they sold to Creole merchants their rafts and baled furs and corn crops (transmogrified to whiskey for convenience in packaging), and walked home.

With the profit from a year's work clanking in their money belts, the rafters stopped off at Natchez-Under-the-Hill for a recuperative romp before the long voyage home. Gamblers, whores, and cutpurses from the ends of the world had gathered to fleece those wooly sheep. Perched on the bluff, a rhythm band of drunken Indians tootled on cane flutes and banged on kettle bottoms to serenade new arrivals. Buzzards patrolled the skies by day and perched onimously by night along the ridgepoles, watching for a suitably lethal riot to break out below.

Those boatmen who escaped Sin City often got skinned on the way home, because they walked 500 miles up the Natchez Trace to Nashville exposed all the way to bands of vicious highwaymen who seldom left living witnesses to testify against them.

Natchez was the far outpost of what was then called the Southwest Frontier. Founded by the French in 1716, even before New Orleans, the

Having already created America's liveliest restored historical section in town, the citizens of Natchez moved downstairs to the notorious stews of Natchez-Under-the-Hill where they are recreating a tamer version of the river boatman's playground.

Natchez fell to the Union Army with scarcely an angry shot, so the grand quarters of antebellum aristocracy were saved for later generations.

city on the bluffs hoisted flags in a bewildering series of exchanges negotiated overseas between Spain, France, and England. At the outbreak of the Revolution, Natchez happened to be flying the British flag, but the population was, at best, indifferent to the distant struggle on the Atlantic seaboard. A Gallup Poll taken at the time would probably have shown 15 percent Tory, 60 percent Couldn't Care Less, and 25 percent getting rest and recreation at Natchez-Under-the-Hill and unavailable for comment.

The Spanish took advantage of England's preoccupation with the pesky colonists on the Atlantic Coast and seized the Natchez District. Manuel Gayoso de Lerma fortified the bluffs there and at Walnut Hills which became Vicksburg and at Chickasaw Bluff which today is Memphis. Manuel Gayoso was a brilliant administrator, a cunning conspirator who tried to separate all the transmontane west as far north as Kentucky from the newly-forming United States, a tireless urban planner and builder and, by all contemporary accounts, a most charming man. In Natchez the church, other public buildings, and many old residences built during his benign rule still stand. So do scores of other houses built in the prosperous era he left behind on 30 March 1798 when the Spanish sailed away and a corporal's guard of American soldiers raised the new flag.

Natchez-Under-the-Hill was almost entirely swept away when the river changed course through a cutoff

and carried away the lowland that had harbored a race track, gambling hells, brothels, and a few places of downright bad repute. Today, a start has been made at re-creating a resort with pleasant restaurant services and divers other small enterprises. The nearest the riverfront strip ever gets to the rousing old days, however, is when the *Mississippi Queen* ties up, and the floating jazz band repairs to a suitably ratty-looking saloon for a jam session. Tame stuff compared to the knifings and shootings and boozy riotings of an earlier day, but it will do.

During the Depression, the desperate women of Natchez looked about for something they could sell to tide them over till good times returned, if ever. They decided that the very houses they inhabited were the most salable treasures they were likely to uncover. Led by Mrs. J. Balfour Miller, they organized the annual Pilgrimages when thousands troop through the old mansions. Year-round a few houses rotate the duty of staying open for a steady stream of tourists curious about the stuff the cotton nabobs embellished their domestic lives with before Naugahyde and Formica and chromium trim brought functionalism to the decorator's service.

Natchez has an embarrassment of riches in historic architectural treasures. Everywhere through the town are delightfully restored cottages that haven't been listed for official tours. The downtown is steadily

When the rest of the United States was bulldozing its antiquated buildings to make room for modern tourist attractions, the ladies of Natchez were ferociously protecting their old structures. Now the tourists flock to Natchez by the tens of thousands.

93

Horse's hoof and wagon wheel wore down the Natchez Trace during forty years of emigration to what was then the Southwest Frontier. The wilderness has long since been tamed to a gentle land of gardens and pastures.

being rescued from some misguided modernization of a few years past.

Natchez is beautiful. Square foot for square foot, Natchez may be the most encouraging demonstration of community-wide historic preservation in North America.

Land-hungry pioneers who crossed the Appalachians on the way to Natchez and the empty Southwest found a crude road that had first been beaten down by woods buffalo and then adopted by the Indians as a reasonably dry pathway. Eventually it was called the Natchez Trace. During the closing decades of the eighteenth century and the beginning of the nineteenth, along its 500-mile route every year 20,000 pioneers came down from the North or boatmen walked home from New Orleans.

When Natchez grew big enough to have serious business with the Federals in the East, local businessmen persuaded the army to cut the brush along the road so that they could send and receive government mail overland instead of by the tedious water journey down the river and across the seas.

In 1800 a festive crowd gathered to welcome the first mail delivery by the new route. Bands greeted the first post rider at King's Tavern—which still stands, incidentally, as the oldest building in town. The city's governors gathered around the postmaster as he opened the first official pouch of the new postal service. Inside was a soggy pudding of letters and dispatches, all that remained of the shipment after weeks of being dragged through swampland and overflowing bayous.

There was a normal six-week delay between mail arrivals in those hardy times and occasionally the postmaster had to announce that there would be no mail at all because "the rider is presumed lost" to robbers or drowning.

With half a continent thrown open to Americans in 1803 after the Louisiana Purchase, a steady parade of pioneers wore down the soft loess of the Trace till the road had sunk so deep that a horse and wagon full of hopeful pioneers could pass unseen by observers on the surface.

Today long stretches of the old route have become a national park. After more than half a century of promises, several short stretches remain incompleted, but the Natchez Trace is nevertheless one of America's most delightful parks—a leisurely drive through landscaping by plantings so artfully done that scarcely a commercial building or other sign of modern Mississippi appears along the route. Motorists drive for miles before they realize that the eerie feeling the landscape gives them is caused by a total lack of billboards.

Here and there beside the paved road are preserved vestiges of the Old Trail, deep trenches pounded down so hard by the wagon wheels of a century and a half ago that trees still can't push through the packed earth.

Ethel Mohamed of Belzoni felt the mysterious stirrings of the creative artist that afflict one in a thousand. She turned to the needle, a medium made familiar to her by the demands of a large family. Today her works are widely celebrated and in demand—but totally out of circulation for she will not surrender them for any appeal, much less for money.

Along the way also are a restored early tavern at Mount Locust, historic-site markers, picnic areas with free firewood, and campsites.

There is plenty of material for historic plaques along the Trace and the countryside it served.

Just six miles east of Natchez at Washington stand

Descendants of the pioneers who supplanted the Indians return to the Trace for a session by a campfire, as though to satisfy some atavistic longing. The few Choctaws who escaped forced emigration cook their SOFKEE and work at their ancient crafts within walking distance of the Trace that brought in the invaders who displaced their ancestors.

the buildings of Jefferson Military College. Jefferson Davis supposedly studied there before going to West Point, and a persistent but unverified legend reports that Audubon gave drawing lessons. The state constitution was drawn up there, and Aaron Burr sat under the immense spreading oaks at a pretrial hearing on a charge of treason—for which the grand jury could find no evidence, incidentally, though he was held anyhow by the judge, apparently for the crime of having evil thoughts. Burr dawdled away his arrest time in Natchez as the lion of a society that only a short generation before had been seditiously anti-American by the lights of the Eastern Establishment.

Maj. Gen. Andrew Jackson encamped his 2,070 Tennessee militiamen near Washington on his march to guard New Orleans against the British early in the War of 1812. It was there that he received a disconcerting command from national headquarters to disband his force 500 miles from home without providing pay or supplies.

Jackson seized wagons to transport his sick, bought provisions out of his own pocket, gave his own mounts to ailing soldiers, and walked the long way home. It was then the common folk began to call him Old Hickory.

Grant landed his troops near the site where Andrew

In the sparsely settled land between Port Gibson and the river stand the columns of Windsor, all that remains of the most magnificent planter's mansion of the countryside after a fire started by a cigarette-smoking visitor. A humble cabin now occupies the spot in a shift of scenery that would be too pat even for William Faulkner to use as a symbol for the fall of the mighty.

Jackson had once run a grocery store and race track and slave trading post at Bruinsburg. He moved swiftly up the sunken roads, shrouded in perpetual gloom by trees that meet overhead, and a perfect setting for an ambush from the high banks on either side—a trap the Confederates failed to spring which failure cost them Vicksburg and with it, the war.

The countryside has a spooky remoteness now, and it is not surprising to come across the Ruins of Windsor, five-story columns standing in a pasture, all that remain of the grandest country mansion for a hundred miles around when it burned in 1890. The owner's son, who was a seven-year-old boy at the fire, told me that it was started by a young house guest who flicked a cigarette into a corner of the ballroom.

The Trace barely bypasses Port Gibson, a "hotbed of tranquility" that General Grant, according to legend, pronounced too beautiful to burn. Considering Grant's brutal destruction of vast areas of the South elsewhere, a skeptic can suspect that Grant was in a frantic sweat to grab Vicksburg and that the town's undoubted beauty had little weight in his decision to move along without taking time to strike a match. In any case, the tree-shaded streets of beautifully-tended antebellum cottages are a pleasant frame for the famous Presbyterian Church with the golden finger pointing heavenward.

At Jackson, the Trace is interrupted by a 30,000-acre reservoir backed up by a dam across the Pearl River.

Kosciusko honors the "George Washington of Poland" who also labored mightily for American freedom from royal oppression.

Up the Trace at French Camp Academy is the carriage that Greenwood Leflore, the quarter-breed chief of the Choctaws, supposedly rode in to Washington to ask Andrew Jackson to remove a crooked Indian superintendent. Legend says that Andrew Jackson thundered at Leflore, "As President of the United States, I tell you the man is not a crook." To which Leflore answered in equally imperious tones, "And as chief of the Choctaw Nation, I tell you he is a scoundrel and has to go."

Jackson won in the end, however, for he put such pressure on the Choctaw Nation that Leflore eventually presided over the signing of Dancing Rabbit Treaty in 1830 that stripped his people of their lands and drove them to an unknown home in far-off Oklahoma. Descendants of the few diehard Choctaws left behind still make a precarious living east of the Trace around Philadelphia and Carthage, but none of them prospered the way their chieftain did.

The Trace gives out beyond Tupelo, except for useless little bits and patches. One day, Mississippians will insist on its completion and then will become full heir to the beautiful thread to the past that buffalo, Indian, and restless pioneer stamped out for us.

Nostalgia buffs can take the Natchez Trace back to World War I in their antique cars. And the real students of bygone days can travel back truly far in time at the Petrified Forest where the trees are millions of years old.

When cattle in vast herds moved to Mississippi to escape western drouths, cowboy skills came with them. Today, the cutting horse champion is most likely to be from Mississippi rather than from the Western ranges.

Only about once a decade does the Mississippi forest put on a colorful autumn show, but the faithful sweet gum does its assigned task of jazzing up the October landscape every year, for which it earns high honors.

Homer Garza, an Apache Indian dancer, was lured by Jackson's fast rise in the ballet world to move from western mesas to the Mississippi lowlands.

One of the state's major resources has always been its artists. Beverly Lowry, along with hundreds of other writers, dancers, singers, painters, sculptors and composers, has shown the world that Mississippi is a place that fosters the creative spirit.

CHAPTER 7

Jackson, the Capital

MISSISSIPPI'S CAPITAL rambled restlessly during the years of territory and early statehood—leaving Natchez for Washington, for instance, with a brief interlude at Columbia, from where the legislature sent a three-man commission up the Pearl River to find a suitable spot somewhere near the geographic center of the state. The trio settled on LeFleur's Bluff, a trading post run by a French-Canadian, standing at what is now South State and Silas Brown Streets, where the Pearl River comes closest to the railroad tracks. It was a reasonable choice, for the Pearl River had been good to LeFleur by bringing him the frontier commerce that moved more easily over watercourses than along tangled woodland paths.

The commissioners missed the center of the state by about fifty miles, however, for it is on the Natchez Trace not far from Ofahoma (which means "red dog" in Choctaw).

In 1821, the legislature commissioned a Peter Van Dorn and an Abraham DeFrance, superintendent of public buildings in Washington, D.C., to plat a city for public service according to plans supposedly suggested seventeen years earlier by that gifted busybody Thomas Jefferson. Laid out as a checkerboard, the city alternated building squares with parks. Though most of the parks have vanished, ghosts of the open spaces still remain; Jackson's downtown is not squeezed quite so painfully into a few towering skyscrapers and narrow traffic-infested streets surrounded by a vast low-lying city of ample spaces as are some other metropolitan centers.

Green space still abounds. In the residential districts, real estate developers have violated the basic law of their craft by letting mature trees stand instead of bulldozing everything green and then naming the naked streets for trees and flowers.

Andrew Jackson himself spoke in his namesake city in 1840, but even that ferocious defender of the Union was not able to dampen separationist sentiment and by 1861 the Secession Convention, meeting in what is now the Old Capitol, voted to leave.

When Jackson's founders laid out the city, they left a park on every alternate block. The parks have largely disappeared but the open space has remained, giving the city an airy open skyline, less architecturally imposing than some but eminently sensible and comfortable.

109

In the heart of Jackson stands the imposing and rapidly expanding campus of Jackson State University, the largest predominantly black school for leagues around. James Perkins, Ph.D., leads his students through problems in physics and chemistry so tangled that, to the uninitiated, he might as well be speaking Sanskrit. Melvin Miller's job is guarding the good name of Jackson State by seeing that the world hears about the best that is happening there.

As the political center of the state, Jackson had also inevitably become the intellectual, commercial, and cultural center. When Grant decided to lop the legs off the Confederacy by cutting the West away from the East, his first surgery was the excision of the Rebel river fortress at Vicksburg. Once that radical amputation was accomplished, he cauterized a belt back of the city to insure that the Confederacy's torso on the Eastern seaboard was grievously mutilated and dying. As the very nerve center of Mississippi, Jackson was the plexus where Grant could paralyze the Rebel midriff. He turned loose General William Tecumseh Sherman with orders to destroy the capital city. In a brisk warm-up for his March to the Sea a little more than a year later, Sherman levelled the city.

"We have made fine progress today in the work of destruction," he wrote his boss Grant. "Jackson will no longer be a point of danger. The land is devastated for thirty miles around."

Because the bricks and rocks of their flues were all that survived the burning of the houses, Jackson became known as Chimneyville.

The exhausting grind ended for everybody at Appomattox in 1865, and Jackson began rebuilding. The intellectual world was restored as quickly as any other. As life resumed, Tougaloo College and what is now Jackson State University, began teaching. By the end of the century, Millsaps College had opened its doors. Then came Belhaven College, and finally the immense complex that has grown up around the University of Mississippi Medical School, founded in 1955.

So Jackson has a patchwork of campuses scattered about. The grounds at Tougaloo on the outskirts of the city are wooded and restful. Belhaven and Millsaps are oases of quiet walks under shade trees within sight of city streets. Jackson State is a surprisingly large and crowded campus studded with new construction in the heart of the city. And the medical school is a gigantic constellation of new structures housing health services, hospitals, schools, clinics, and laboratories, teeming with research technicians, nurses, computer programmers, medical students, doctors, and parking lot security guards.

Understandably, Millsaps makes much of its selection by *The New York Times Selective Guide to Colleges* as the only advanced school from Mississippi listed among the 265 colleges and universities recommended by the authors out of more than 3,000 advanced educational institutions in the United States. Academically, it was rated on a par with Tulane, Southern Methodist, and Purdue; socially, with Davidson, Emory, and Harvard; and in quality of life with Dartmouth, Grinnell, and Princeton.

Historically, Millsaps has a harder-won distinction. It was the first white Mississippi college voluntarily to abolish racial barriers, a move that at its time required

111

At tiny Millsaps University, rated by a prestigious study among the 265 top schools out of more than 3,000, students and instructors welcome February's first warm spell under flowering trees. The giant of Jackson's educational complex is Dr. Arthur Guyton at the University of Mississippi Medical Center. Acknowledged by most of the world's physicians to be the finest living physiologist, Dr. Guyton has written a textbook that teaches the world's medical students from Mississippi's capital.

a courage unrecognized by the generation that has grown up since.

A few blocks away at the bustling mid-city campus of Jackson State University, I met James Perkins, Ph.D., head of the chemistry department and chairman of the division of natural sciences.

Speaking in a hard Pennsylvania accent that cut like a diamond through the soft Afro-Southern voices that surrounded him on the black campus, Dr. Perkins explained the workings of a dozen Buck Rogers contraptions. He and his faculty use them to pursue research projects in chemistry and physics so far beyond man's poor senses that mathematical formulas bristling with Greek letters and strange punctuation marks replace sight, sound, taste, and smell.

A walk through the University of Mississippi medical complex offered no relief from the rarefied altitude of Jackson's intellectual stratosphere.

Working in a shabby office so small it literally does not have enough wall space to accommodate just his international awards, Dr. Arthur Guyton punches out on a computer terminal mathematical questions about the body's functions. He relays the electronic brain's answers to a waiting medical world.

Because his studies in physiology have ventured so deep into the human body's constellation of interlocking, overlapping, and interacting systems, each of dizzying complexity, Dr. Guyton now works in a realm beyond language. Only mathematics can probe further into the shadowy depths where he is pursuing truths.

Using 400 equations governing the cardiovascular system, for instance, he constructs on the computer screen a model of the human body that looks like a stock market analysis. Tapping the keyboard, he slightly impairs kidney function, somewhat increases salt consumption and measures the long-range increase in cardiac output leading to a rise in blood pressure. A model with normal kidney function and the same increase in salt intake shows little effect.

In seconds, instead of years, using a few microwatts of electricity instead of thousands of laboratory animals and human volunteers, Dr. Guyton has suggested that salt is the villain in hypertension only among those with impaired kidney function. Lab tests will later confirm the machine's prediction, but medicine already has inched forward.

Dr. Guyton is ranked by most of his colleagues as

Even Mississippians are startled to learn that the first heart and lung transplants were performed in their capital by Dr. James Hardy. Despite awesome research and administrative duties, Dr. Hardy operates daily on the theory that a surgeon's place is in the operating room.

the world's foremost physiologist. His textbook on physiology is the basic study tool for most of the world's medical students. His former pupils run the medicine or physiology staffs in Japan, the Philippines, Holland, Switzerland, Egypt, and all over the United States. Discoveries about bodily functions that come from his inspired computer practice have reshaped medical thinking.

At the cutting edge of the world's cardiovascular surgical research is the center's Dr. James D. Hardy.

Even most Mississippians are startled to learn that the world's first lung and heart transplants were made by Dr. James Hardy and his team in Jackson.

Dr. Hardy does research, administers the department of surgery, writes textbooks, and was president of the American College of Surgeons. But most important, he still operates daily.

"The final act of surgery, after all, is operating," he says. "Our students and residents are here to learn to operate, and I couldn't help them very much if they never saw me in OR."

Dr. Hardy's students have fanned out over Mississippi.

"In 1955, there were only a few board-certified surgeons in the entire state. Now I don't think there's a town of any size at all that doesn't have at least one surgeon who is board-certified. That's largely a result of this institution's work."

Because of the several academies, Jackson is a natural garden for the arts. But highbrows cannot support a healthy art world without help. Romantics picture art flourishing in garrets, but realists know that artists flock where the dollars are. Discovery of oil in the state and concentration of the area's banking in Jackson provided the dollars. The arts were not slow to appear.

With the intellectual and academic community to draw from, the cultural world can count on a reasonably good house. Artists find hospitality for their shows in galleries and even in the lobbies of banks. The Municipal Art Gallery changes its exhibit of regional arts every month. Out at Tougaloo College, the museum staff shows contemporary works including Picasso and Dali augmented by African sculpture and Afro-American art. Jackson State University Museum specializes in local black artists. There is a crafts center at Ridgeland on the Natchez Trace, the Manship House has changing exhibits of the decorative arts, even the Governor's Mansion offers changing exhibits of Mississippi art.

The true nerve center of Mississippi's culture lies in a complex at downtown's south edge that houses an imposing Museum of Art, the Russell C. Davis Planetarium and a Municipal Auditorium that visiting theatre companies find superior to most houses in the world's major theatrical centers. The museum offers a permanent collection of some importance, hosts frequent

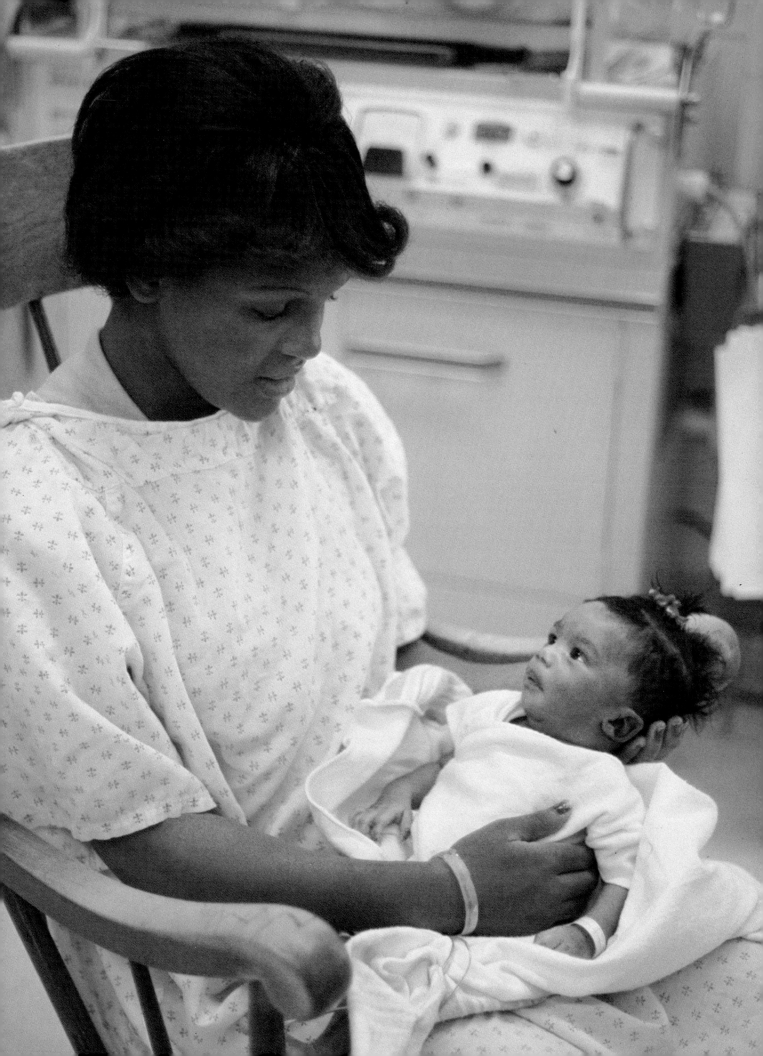

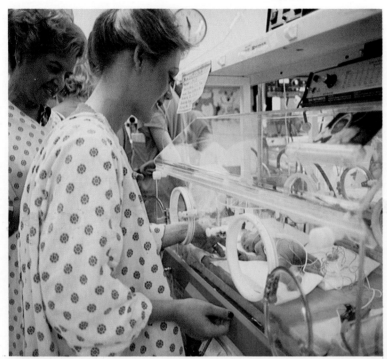

The cat scanner at Jackson's immense medical complex is an impressive tool in medicine's forward march. But far more admired by young mothers is the new art of neonatology which saves prematurely born infants who would not have survived in an earlier day or on a less advanced medical front.

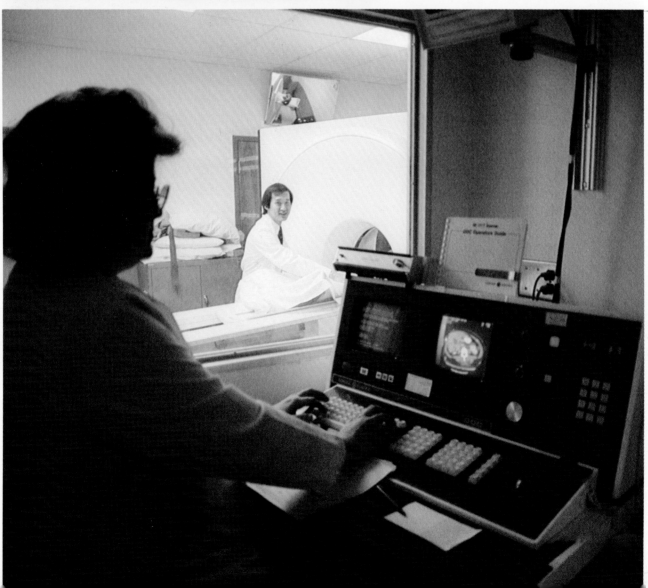

visiting collections, and, what is more important to the
local artist, offers a changing exhibit of local works for
sale. Just to keep the cultural spirits joggled awake,
musicians sometimes hold concerts in the museum or
the planetarium instead of the auditorium.

During May and June every year, office workers
brown-bagging lunch in Smith Park downtown are
entertained by opera students singing arias. Sunday
morning church services are embellished by their voices.
They are brought to Jackson by the Mississippi Opera
Association for an opera festival that includes schools
on set and costume design, children's opera, and performance of some of the great war horses like *Don
Giovanni,* usually with a cast augmented by a few big-
name singers.

The year-round Opera South, a mostly black opera
company, presents a mixed repertoire of standards and
Afro-American works.

Besides its own classical programs, the symphony
orchestra furnishes the musical backbone for virtually
all the visiting stars and also sends musicians to beef
up small symphonies scattered about the state.

But the real dazzlers are the balletomanes. In 1979,
for the first time in history, there came to the Western
Hemisphere the International Ballet Competition—
more or less the world championship of the dance
world. For two weeks, the world's best dancers and
fans followed anxiously the trials at the international
contest. All eyes were focused on Jackson.

"On *where?*" asked an incredulous international press.

"On Jackson . . . Jackson, Mississippi."

Reporters, photographers, television cameramen,
dance critics, and celebrities of the dance world crowded the town. Television commentators and anchormen
on the national networks openly struggled with their
disbelief that they were reporting that world-class cultural happening from Jackson, Mississippi.

But they indisputably were, and they wanted to
know why.

When she retired from the tumultuous New York
dance scene, Thalia Mara, one of ballet's great teachers,
became the artistic director of the Jackson company.
The competition was her inspiration. Because of her
friendship with the greats of the ballet world, she
brought a blue ribbon jury and faculty for a two-week
school that read like *Who's Who.*

Machinery set up since will make Jackson a regular
host to the competition, rotating the duty with such
exotic outposts as Varna, Bulgaria, Tokyo, and Mos-
cow. So every four years, the dance world will focus
on Jackson.

Despite the bulging muscles of the *danseurs* and the
ineffably feminine grace of the ballerinas, a large number of barbarians persist in believing there is something
sexless and wanly effete about ballet. Audiences at the
first International Competition became a corps of pub-

118

licists to spread the word through the state that the dance was one of the most muscular and certainly the sexiest spectator sport on the calendar.

But even the most ardent balletomane must admit that Mississippi's masses more often find recreation in earthier pursuits than the dance. There, too, Jackson serves.

Jackson stunned the dancing world in 1979 by holding the first Ballet International Competition to come to the New World. Since then, the competition has become a regular quadrennial establishment. The world's greatest names in the dance come to judge and teach at the school that accompanies the contest, among them Thalia Mara, (above) Robert Joffrey (far left) and Alexandra Danilova (near left).

119

For the football maniacs, of which there are legions, Jackson's main reason for existence is its stadium. During the off-season, the city does plod along doing the state's governmental and commercial business. Aerial views confirm the motorist's impression that Jackson is airier, more forested, less congested than most capitals, which is a legacy of its founders who planned it that way.

There are the great gladiatorial football clashes of autumn, of course, but Jackson furnishes only the stadium and parking lot for the most prestigious of those. The city's contribution to the state's recreation is probably largest in the conservation of wildlife and fisheries.

David Watts at the Department of Wildlife Conservation plasters his bulletin board and walls with statistical proof of the agency's efficacy in providing game for the state's gunners and fish for the anglers.

"In 1920 the state probably had fewer than 1,500 deer surviving," he said. "Today, because of decades of sound management, Mississippi has well over a million deer."

Hunters bring down more than 200,000 annually, or 13 times as many as existed at the low point. Indeed, as the game department says, "Without large predatory animals that once helped to hold the deer herds in balance with their food supplies, problems often result from too many rather than too few deer."

Whenever any of the state's ranges become over-stocked with deer, the bosses call an antlerless hunt when does and fawns are fair game for the hunters to thin the herds back to the numbers the habitat can support in good health.

Wild turkey went through the same downs-and-ups of population. In 1928 the great Aldo Leopold, who was the prime mover for game management in North America, said about Mississippi, "Wild turkey are steadily decreasing. They have been cleaned out of the upland ranges, and there is barely a seed stock left in the larger swamps."

In the 1950's, the game commission seized on the newly-invented cannon-projected net to trap 2,000 wild turkeys for release in promising but barren habitats about the state. Those few ancestors that had somehow survived to become the seed stock for the state had developed a wiliness that they passed on to their progeny. Mississippi's wild turkeys are probably the most difficult of all the world's game to lure within gunshot range, for they are survivors and suffer none of the stupidity of their domestic cousins. A hunter who can outsmart a wild gobbler can be proud of his own bulging intellect.

Gunners take three million or more squirrels. Nobody can estimate how many rabbits are shot; it's well up in the millions.

Quail populations have been seriously reduced, especially in the Delta, by mechanized clean-farming which leaves little cover for the birds. But doves thrive

Lying almost in the semi-tropics, the state suffers little winter, but the occasional snow storm does confound the residents.

on it. The annual harvest of doves is prodigious. Experts will not estimate how many fall each year but agree it is an astronomical number. And every following year the doves are back in their teeming millions.

The wood duck, undoubtedly the snappiest dresser of the waterfowl world, has also come back from near extinction, largely because of a nest box program set up by the commission to replace the hollow trees they once nested in. Commission sanctuaries planted with Japanese millet, soybeans, corn, and smartweed give immense migratory flocks of all species of North American waterfowl feeding and resting room. About 30,000 hunters fill their bags, especially in the Delta and other lowland regions.

Game fishing, always good, has only been improved by impoundment of rivers behind dams. But even among game fish, there is a cliff-hanger in the struggle to escape extinction. The striped bass, an anadromous fish that swims back and forth from brackish to fresh water, was almost wiped out by industrial pollution. The commission cleaned up industry's act and re-stocked the striper's original home streams. Carried away by their success, the commission went on to stock reservoirs that held only fresh water. The fish flourished.

Leafing through the bales of bulletins pinned to his wall, Watts reported, "The biggest striper was a thirty-two-pounder taken at Grenada. But thirty-pounders are caught every year at Barnett. And whoppers come out of Sardis and Okatibee."

Alligators reintroduced by the commission are doing great, Watts said. Without any help from anybody, beavers are also staging a spectacular comeback, so spectacular, in fact, that farmers hold beaver control meetings to exchange desperate advice on how to keep the manicly busy engineers from flooding the state's best pasturelands.

Unbeknownst to hunters, the commission's thinkers in Jackson have come up with a new scheme to stock the state's forests and fields.

"We found a strain of ring-necked pheasants in Texas that is used to hot and humid weather," Watts said. "We are tentatively releasing some of those birds to see if they can take our climate. If they catch on, hunters will have another sport for the autumn days."

Ardent environmentalists have their niche reserved in the Museum of Natural Science where changing exhibits, films, and workshops teach the interdependence of life.

And for those who like their animal exhibits to be round and breathing, there is always the Jackson Zoo where the staff is doing advanced work in preserving the genetic diversity of its endangered species by cooperative breeding programs with other institutions. Jackson has chosen the cheetah as its key species for preservation from extinction.

*The state's recreation largely happens somewhere out of doors. Horseman-
ship standards are high, competitions keen. Scattered about the state are
vast reservoirs impounded behind dams. Ross Barnett Reservoir brings boat-
ing mania to deeply landlocked Jackson.*

Outdoor amusements range from the coon hunt for the good old boys to the fox hunt for the pink coat set. A stirrup cup speeds all manner of hunters into the field from a heady Montrachet at the Canton fox hunt to a fizzy Coca Cola at French Camp.

When the young Choctaw dancers came off their home grounds to dance for the first time on the outside during the First International Ballet Competition, young maidens of widely different cultures discover they share a love for the dance.

When the world-famed Dane Peter Martins worked out an experimental dance program, he tried it out on the balletomane Mississippi public at Biloxi. His tumultuous reception led him, and his partner Mikhail Baryshnikov, to take the ground breaking performance to the White House.

131

CHAPTER 8

The Delta

T HE MISSISSIPPI DELTA begins in the lobby of the
  Peabody Hotel in Memphis and ends on Catfish Row
in Vicksburg.''

That inspired sentence is a clear steal from David Cohn's
God Shakes Creation, of course, but why should I be prouder than
William Faulkner who unwittingly committed the same larceny by stealing
Cohn's immortal line to open the only nonfiction piece the Nobel Laureate
ever wrote about Mississippi? As his unconscious memory told Faulkner,
the sentence has the economy of line and inevitability of form that makes
a brilliant-cut diamond beautiful. It's a line *worth* stealing.

Every Mississippian knows the Delta, of course, but outlanders are usually bewildered because the Mississippi Delta they learned about in school
lies in Southern Louisiana at the mouth of the river.

Mississippi's Delta is a misnamed half moon of lowland stretching along
the river from near Memphis to near Vicksburg and reaching inland to
beyond Greenwood. It is vaguely deltoid in shape and measures about one
hundred sixty miles north to south and fifty miles at the deepest east-west
point. It is rimmed by a cliff which marks the farthest point of the true
North American continent. Till very recent geological times, the Gulf of
Mexico rolled over the Delta and lapped against that escarpment.

In those days—not more than 10,000 or 12,000 years ago—a mile-high
ice cap lay across the top of the world, reaching mid-Missouri and Ohio.
When it melted, a flood poured down the central trough of the continent,
carrying unimaginable tons of gravel and mud. The river's burden dropped
out as the current slowed, building an ever-shallower bed. As the glacier
retreated, the river shrank but continued to meander across a vast flood
plain, dropping its load of sand, clay, and silt. The minerals of an immensely broad and immensely rich region filled the shallows, driving the Gulf of
Mexico southward. The richest deposits fell on the Mississippi Delta. It
rose slowly above the waters and now forms a permanent part of the Mississippi landscape.

*Flat as a pool table, stripped virtually bald to
make room for incredible crops of wheat, soybeans
and cotton, the Delta landscape offers little excitement; ergo, the folk who inhabit the insipid
country have to provide the spice that makes life
worth living. Which they do by being light-hearted,
improvident, feckless, pleasure-obsessed, and generous. They are superb farmers and terrible businessmen. You couldn't stand them if they weren't
so likable.*

133

There have been winter days when I did not think we need wait until the great meltdown for a return of the Gulf of Mexico, after an absence of ten millennia. The Delta gets what even conservative meteorologists admit is 55 inches of rain a year. But any Deltan would swear that the rainfall must run closer to 550 inches, most of it in February and March.

Indians made some small use of the slightly elevated banks beside the Delta's bayous to establish rather civilized colonies of the Mississippi Culture sent from the Indian Vatican at Cahokia, a huge town across the Mississippi from where St. Louis now stands. The Winterville Mound cluster was probably the regional cathedral served by satellite temples atop mounds scattered everywhere in the lowlands. Archeologists insist they were erected as temple sites and not as refuges

during high water, though we can assume that the aborigines did not hesitate to climb the slopes to keep from getting their moccasins wet in the regular springtime overflows.

When the first white men came to the Southwest Frontier, they found the Delta still too new and wet a geological development for farming, a morass fit only for snakes and alligators till further silt deposit and a bit of artificial drainage had dried out some of the river bottom swamp.

The first planters began to trickle in well after the first decades of the nineteenth century. The cotton boom that followed invention of the gin brought prosperity to the pioneer planters, but at great cost in labor and health.

When the Civil War ended the great days of cotton

prosperity, the white civilization of the Delta was scarcely a generation old. That's why there are few antebellum houses or monuments in the lowlands.

The white mistresses of the pioneer plantations came from the established societies of Kentucky and the Virginia and Carolina tidewater country. So did the black women, though on a different social level. White and black, they suffered the rude shock of leaving tranquil Eastern households for the turbulent life of a harsh frontier. The whites moved from colonnaded mansions to log cabins, the blacks from brick hutches to wattle and daub shanties of unspeakable squalor.

Snakes abounded. So did bears and wolves. As late as 1867, a party of Greenville hunters tethered a goat under blinds built in trees and shot down enough wolves to form what one of the hunters reported was "a levee of their dead bodies three and four feet high." A modern reader who knows a little something about wolves can suspect a hunter's tall tale in that colorful levee of bodies, but the gunmen probably did kill a goodly number. Maybe as many as two or three, if they shot fast enough before the grey ghosts melted back into the brush.

But the most heart-wringing trial of those pioneer women must have been the swamp fevers that ravaged their families. Deadly malaria was more commonplace in those days than heartburn is now. Mothers had to suffer the agony of watching husbands and children shiver themselves first into ghastly skeletonized wraiths and then into their graves. Yellow jack swept over the swamps every few years, carrying off entire families to the last soul, or even more cruelly, leaving the mother to contemplate the ruin of her hearth.

Through their pain, the women kept steadily building a civilization. They first had their log houses sheathed with siding—the Erwin house on Lake Washington, probably the oldest house in Washington County, still hides a log substructure under the shiplap exterior—and then had their men build proper houses, modelled after the prim Victorian structures of older regions.

So fertile is the region that even the aboriginal red man developed a high civilization based on agriculture. The immense temple mounds they left behind were paid for by rich crops of maize and squash just as today's cotton and rice support a life style somewhat racier than most farm communities enjoy.

White chatelaines taught black servants how to prepare the victuals the fields and forests provided; black women subtly Africanized the cuisine. Soon, the most aristocratic Southern whites thought that the ultimate in refined dining was the same pork chops, turnip greens greasy with fatback drippings, and corn bread that their field hands ate in their cabins.

Civilization came to the swamp, survived the Civil War, triumphed over the Great Flood of 1927, and lives today.

There have been changes of course, but some are more apparent than real. Prohibition is gone, for instance, but drinking habits have hardly changed, for the law was always a joke in the Delta. Even the legal dealer of today is quite often the illegal pusher of the past. To this day, older Deltans still speak of "going to the bootlegger," when they are headed for the perfectly respectable merchant who has a state license for selling hootch.

Other aspects of the Delta culture haven't changed. Cohn talks about the hospitality of the Delta, about the visits planned for overnight that stretch to weeks— to months—to years.

Deltans still pass house guests from family to family as though they were precious commodities, reluctantly given on loan. The occasional foreigner who strays into the Delta finds himself snapped up by eager hostesses, made the pretext for several of the endless parties Deltans live for, and reluctantly allowed to return home only after leaving his address and promising to write often.

Little does the innocent foreigner understand the perils of leaving an address with a Delta hostess. For the rest of his life, he is condemned to finding on the other end of his telephone in Europe, or Asia, or Africa, a sweet Southern voice announcing brightly that his old friend from the Delta is in town and would dearly love to see him.

For generations, Deltans have told merchants and bankers that they would pay their debts "when the gin whistle blows," and the year's cotton money comes in. Cotton is no longer king, and the gin whistle no longer signals the sole annual influx of money. Soybeans bring in more money than cotton, and speculative advance sale of newly-planted cotton crops spreads income over the year. But the habits persist. In the Delta, having fun is more important than keeping the creditor happy.

Deltans enjoy telling visitors an apocryphal story about a New York banking executive sent to Clarksdale to collect a million-dollar debt long overdue. He was sucked up into the plantation social whirl and disappeared from the view of his bosses. Weeks later, in answer to their frantic telegrams, he wired them back:

"Forget the million dollars. Forward all mail to my new address down here. These folks know how to live."

The arts have flourished only feebly in the Delta culture. Greenville enjoyed a small flutter of literary activity for a few years, but most of the writers died like Hodding Carter and David Cohn and William Alexander Percy. Or they moved away like Walker Percy, Shelby Foote, Charles Bell, and Beverly Lowry. Ellen Douglas and I remain, but we moved here from elsewhere.

The artists who have come from the Delta to galvanize large sections of the world are black blues singers.

W.C. Handy led the way by playing for country club dances around Cleveland before moving to Memphis where he made his name with *St. Louis Blues* and *Memphis Blues.*

The list of world-famed singers who have followed seems endless: B.B. King of Indianola, Son House of Cleveland, Jimmy Reed and Son Thomas of Leland, Howling Wolf of Clarksdale, Little Milton, Charlie Patton and Hound Dog Taylor of Greenville, the Turners of Clarksdale, Otis Stann of Belzoni, Mississippi John Hurt of Greenwood, John Lee Hooker and Muddy Waters from Rolling Fork, and the granddaddy of them all, Robert Johnson of Yazoo City.

A white singer named Johnny Winters of Leland has sneaked into the black company. Charley Pride of Sledge has become a giant on the country and western scene where few other blacks even venture. Bruce Blackman of Greenville composes songs that sell enough records to pave the Delta.

The cachet of being from the Delta is so great that a certain singer named McDowell has set up for business in Como and calls himself Mississippi Fred. But insiders know he's really from Tennessee.

I am a writer and my entire factory is the size of a portable typewriter. I can live anywhere in the world I wish. Nevertheless, I wouldn't live anywhere in the world but on this sun-blistered mud flat.

Why?

Well, my neighbors are more often kind than cruel; they are *never* indifferent. They are feckless and improvident, but unrestrainedly generous. They hold an artist in a vague kind of respect. They never return anything they borrow, but on the other hand, they'll give you the shirts off their backs.

I don't know why, but I love them.

Charm has always been the reason for being of the young Mississippi girl. Pre-party strategy sessions in the boudoir laid out campaigns that hapless males fell victim to without even knowing the tactical plans existed and had been flawlessly executed.

*Soybeans have recently replaced cotton in dollars
earned and in acres planted, but tradition dies
hard and cotton is still king in the Delta mind.*

For the substantial portion of the Delta's population that depends on nature's vagaries for a living, one of the most exciting days of the year is the morning the first cotton plant bursts from the fecund earth to feed on the hot spring sun.

142

Two of the manufacturing moguls of the Delta:
Lee McCarty of Merigold shapes Mississippi mud
into highly salable pottery and Charles Bannerman
shapes capital and managerial skills into an
interstate network of industrial enterprises.

Even more than cotton, what has won the Delta world renown is its export of blues singers. Every September they return to Greenville for a festival to celebrate the art which is virtually a Delta monopoly." Among the giants appearing are Sam Chatman (far left) and Napoleon Strickland (near left.)

Young folk know how to savor life. In the past,
more than one child held still for a scalp punish-
ing session with comb and brush for the reward of
a Saturday trip to town. There, a guitar man
sang a "blues" to celebrate a weekend, sheltered
from the brutal cotton field sun. James "Son"
Thomas of Leland has carried his art across
oceans to astound the folk of other lands with
folk music from the Delta's cotton fields.

150

As the sharecropper left the land for the big city, many small Delta towns faded. These symbols of the past have now given way to a bright and hopeful future for the state.

Joy Guravich works through a thicket at Leroy Percy State Park searching for new species during the Christmas Bird Count of the Audubon Society.

Everybody has troubles, but on a sunny January day the nearby tropics sneak through the back door and Mississippians blossom in the mid-winter warmth.

To keep the arts alive, throughout history some have had to teach and some have had to support. Malcolm Norwood nurtures the talents he finds at Delta State University. Mary Jayne Whittington's helping hand reaches from Greenwood to the farthest corners of the state in furthering the cause of art.

*Old hound dog's bugling can call many a lawyer
and commercial man from the dreary business of
running the county's affairs to a day's walk in
the woods.*

CHAPTER 9

Home Again

TRAVEL IS my business. I have visited something like one hundred twenty countries. I've long since lost count because some of the countries I have visited are now two or three countries and some have disappeared. When hearthbound Deltans gush at me how they envy my life, the exciting voyages, the faraway lands with strange-sounding names, the exotic people and their delightfully scandalous customs, I have to go along, for it *is* fun. I wouldn't do anything else, and I can't imagine why everybody is not a writer. But it can be wearing. And lonely. Desperately lonely. It's then that I yearn for a little less excitement and a lot more Mississippi.

Homeward bound from some foreign shore, I stagger into Memphis airport with stubbled chin and bloodshot eyes. Sour humored though I be, Mississippi begins to work its magic the instant I hear those soft feminine accents spoken nowhere but between Memphis and Biloxi. I search for the speakers and there they are—Mississippi women en route somewhere, cool, graceful, chic, as even the Parisienne could not manage in this climate. I am almost home.

On the drive across the Mississippi countryside, it is spring. Around oxbow lakes, wood ducks flash through cypress brakes seeking nesting sites. Fat cows graze in pastures yellow-carpeted with wild ranunculus. A shower melts the earth's winter crust, and cotton sprouts burst through for a first touch of the hot Mississippi sun. Soybean seedlings draw emerald streaks across brown fields flat as a pool table. The pale green of rice, just burst from seed, dusts serpentine levees that writhe across fields fresh torn from lowland woods.

If I am lucky enough to spend the summer at home, I join the planter in watching the sky for needed rain, because I too work that incredibly fertile soil. While my writing colleagues in New York are eating expense-account luncheons of the eternal coq au vin with vegetables that have been traveling for a week across the continent, I carry up from the garden egg-

Nostalgia for a life that satisfies man's basic needs without jangling his soul has made many an exile find his way home to Mississippi—at least for a visit. The passage of the Lowe twins in their lovingly preserved vintage car can throw the unwary visitor back into his youth . . . at least till he looks in the mirror.

163

plant fruit gleaming like amethysts, tomatoes with the acid bite of new wine, lettuce that snaps under the fingernail like a chip of frozen butter, sprigs of aromatic rosemary and basil, and, above all, the garden prize that no city dweller will ever know—sweet corn still in the milk stage rushed from stalk to boiling pot in thirty seconds.

On the first day of dove season, half the state's males disappear from normal haunts; on the first day of deer hunting, only the lame and halt remain on the job. Frost withers tomato vines but brings rich flavor to mustard and turnip greens. Freezers fill for the festive winter.

Then one afternoon I am working my garden and

my heart leaps up, for overhead I hear that ragged gabbling that calls to the nomad deep inside every man. A skein of wild geese passes over, and my soul goes with them, captive of the same mindless wanderlust.

Weeks later, seated at a screechingly overspiced meal in some unpronounceable heathen city, I ache because I am missing the sweet pleasures of the Mississippi winter. I miss those parties thrown together on the most ridiculous pretext—a Too-Much-Rain Party, or a Drouth Party, or a Thank-Heavens-It's-Thursday-Party. I miss flirting with the beautiful women who understand that game superbly well and rarely let it get out of their control. I miss talking weather and crops with the men.

Most of all, I miss the special civilization that Mississippi women have brought to what was only a few generations ago a wilderness.

After only a few sessions of self-pity in the exile I have imposed on myself, there I am again at Memphis airport with bloodshot eyes, groggy from lack of sleep, but intoxicated with the cool beauty of Mississippi girls, for it means that just twelve miles down the road Mississippi begins and I am almost home again.

168

Even in pietistic and orthodox Mississippi, the occasional eccentric and dissenter are tolerated, even cherished as a colorful thread that gives life to the pattern.

The occasional survivors from the days of bolder architectural adventure give the state's small towns a bit of relief from the turkey-egg-bald monotony of modern building design.

Young Mississippi hopefuls are excruciatingly conscious that the state has already given the world one operatic giant in Leontyne Price. Why not another, wonders every contestant at the Metropolitan Auditions in University. And young dancers know with keen longing that the entire ballet world, once every four years, watches for new talent at the International Ballet Competition in Jackson.

Some Mississippians live outside the corn pone and cotton stereotypes. Near Canton pink-coated fox hunters faithfully observe the traditional ritual that accompanies the pursuit of a furry wraith. In New York many Mississippians have become top fashion models, like Mimi Gould of Leland, or furniture designers like Jonson and Marcius of Greenville, or they have become fixtures of journalism, the theater, television—so many, in fact, that every June the Mississippi picnic brings hundreds of the city's smartest to Central Park.

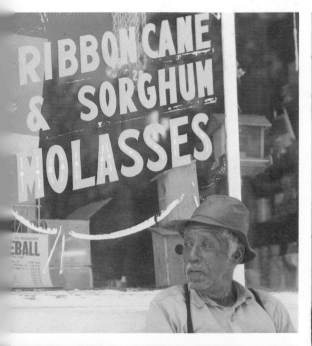

The good Mississippi earth furnishes
a rich table with pecans, catfish and
sorghum molasses.

It is the duty and pleasure of Mississippi's women to teach their younger sisters the feminine graces. One of ballet's great teachers, Thalia Mara, passes along the magic of the dance to Kathy Thibodeaux. And at Florewood State Park, Mary Dabney Dale introduces Somer Rochow to one of the major tools of her craft.

Tranquillity pervades Mississippi life from the depths of a cypress brake to a shady porch.

Photographer's Notes

With few exceptions, the photographs in this book were made with Olympus II cameras using Kodachrome 64 or Hasselblads using Extrachrome 64. Supplementary lighting was added to the ambient light almost never.

More important than the technical data was the warm cooperation the photographer found from all levels of society, white and black, rich and poor, sophisticated and simple. After the suspicion and occasional hostility encountered in other fields, the pleased surprise of Mississippians at being asked to pose was a great relief. The year's work that went into photographing this book was a year's picnic. It would be fun to do it all again.

Gathering the photographs for this book led to delightful excursions to far corners of Mississippi I might have missed in an ordinary lifetime. Unless already indicated in the captions, the locations where photographs were made are as follows:

MISSISSIPPI

Mississippi is published by the University Press of Mississippi and sponsored by the Mississippi Board of Economic Development.

The book was designed by Larry E. Hirst and composed by Hayes Graphic Arts Service, Jackson, Mississippi, using the Goudy Old Style type font. The color separations were supplied by Mississippi Engraving & Color, Inc., also located in Jackson.

The book was printed in Jackson, Mississippi, by Hederman Brothers Printing using Mead basis 100 Offset Black and White Dull paper stock. The press sheets were Smythe-sewn and case-bound in Holliston Roxite C-57590.